THE JESUS CHRIST CHRONICLES

Highlighting the Other Untold True Story
Of the Chief of Travelers, The Messiah!

Compiled and Authored by
WAZIR KOOLOO

Order this book online at www.trafford.com

or email orders@trafford.com

Most Trafford titles are also available at major online book retailers.

Printed in Victoria, BC, Canada.

ISBN: 978-1-4269-2876-5 (sc)

ISBN: 978-1-4269-2875-8 (hc)

Library of Congress Control Number: 2010903040

Our mission is to efficiently provide the world's finest, most comprehensive book publishing service, enabling every author to experience success. To find out how to publish your book, your way, and have it available worldwide, visit us online at www.trafford.com

Trafford rev. 3/4/2010

www.trafford.com

North America & international
toll-free: 1 888 232 4444 (USA & Canada)
phone: 250 383 6864 ♦ fax: 812 355 4082

Contents

Say that which is through it be bitter and displeasing to many.
----- Islam's Holy Prophet, MUHAMMED (u.w.b.p.).

Acknowledgements

I wish to thank Almighty Allah for allowing me the honour to complete a task, which is, completing this book, which has taken me, almost six (6) years to complete – Al laahu ackbar) Allah is the Greatest).

I'm grateful to Suzanne Olsson and Dr. Fida Hassnain for allowing me to use documents and articles, which were obtained from books that they wrote recently; Thanks Again!

The Permissions Department of various Publishing Houses, must be thanked for allowing me permission to highlight various Copyright articles, They're;

Nemonie Craven Roderick of Jonathan Clowes Ltd., for the following:

"Reprinted by kind permission of Jonathon Clowes Ltd., London on behalf of Doris Lessing.|

Anna Murphy of, The Octagon Press Ltd..

Mary Jo Slazak of National Geographic Society Book Division.

Peter London of Harper Collins Publishers (USA).

Rosemarie Cerminaro of Simon & Schuster (Atria Books).

Mrs. Catherine Trippett of Random House (UK).

Emma Richmond-Watson of Harper Collins (UK).

TO YOU ALL THANKS!

A special Salaams to, The Islamic Research Foundation of India for allowing me the honour of mentioning, Dr. Zakir Naik's name in this publication-Thanks!

Another special thanks goes to my sister, Acklima; hey sis! Thanks for loaning me the typewriter!

And to my 'friends' at browwwsers Computer and Internet Café, of San Fernando, South Trinidad (and Tobago), Thanks for the assistance!

If I forgot anyone, I'm sorry, but thank you, thank you and thank you!!!

INTRODUCTION

Perhaps there is no other individual of any prominence in the history of religion about whom so many differences exist as about Jesus. Son of Mary and Joseph –the carpenter, may Hod be pleased with them both.

The Jews, the Christians and the Muslims and hold different views about the birth of Jesus, and the manner of his death.

On the account of his birth, the Christians believed that Jesus was born of the Immaculate Conception, preached and gave his life on the cross to save mankind from sin, was resurrected on the third (3rd) day of ascended to heaven.

The Jews believed that he died an accursed death on the cross.

The Majority of Muslims believed that his birth was a miracle, and that he was never placed on the cross. It was somebody else that resembled Jesus who was crucified, while Jesus was lifted bodily to the heavens, where he is still awaiting the time, when he would return to earth, slay the Dajjal and reunite the Muslim Ummah.

To these Muslims, I ask:

1. Which Verse of the Holy Qur'an states specifically that Jesus ascended to the heavens bodily and will descend bodily and will descend bodily in the latter days?

2. How old will he be then? Did he eat, drink and answer the call of nature? The Holy Qur'an states in Chapter 36, Verse 68:

"And whomsoever We cause to live long, We reduce to an abject state in creation.

Do they not understand?

3. Jesus did not speak Arabic, so how will he communicate and disseminate the message of Islam to the Islamic nations? If he did, then who taught him?

The Holy Qur'an states in Chapter 14, Verse 04:

"And We sent no messenger but with the language of his people, so that he might explain to them clearly. Then Allah leaves in error whom He pleases and He guides whom he pleases. And He is the Mighty, the Wise."

The Islamic Sect called Ahmaddiyya of which there is two "Houses", The Qadiani Ahmadi Muslims, who accept the belief that Jesus was born of a miraculous nature, spent his missing years in the East, proclaimed and preached the Gospel, was put on the cross, but did not die. He fell into a swoon, was taking down form the cross alive, placed into a sepulcher, where an historic ointment, known as the Marham-i-Isa or the Ointment of Jesus was applied to his wounds. Thus recovering from his wounds, he then migrated to the countries where the Lost Tribes of Israel had settled. After preaching and proclaiming the word of God to the inhabitants of Kashmir, he died at the age of 120, and his Tomb, the Rauzabal Mausoleum is located at Srinagar.

The Lahori Ahamid Muslims, also believed in the above mentioned facts, excluding his birth. This branch of Muslims believe that Jesus' Mother Mary married Joseph the Carpenter. After they were married, consummation took place and Prophet Jesus was conceived, some months thereafter.

The Lahori Ahmadi Muslims, also believe that Prophet Jesus, spent his missing years in India. Upon his return to the Holy Land, he was hiven Divine Instructions to preach the Injeel or Gospel to the children of Israel. His Ministry lasts some three (3) years. He was betrayed, arraingned and Tried for Blasphemy.

He was placed on the cross on a Friday Afternoon, survived the Crucifixion after falling into the swoon, was taken down alive and placed in a sepulcher, where the Marham-i-Isa was applied to his wounds.

After recovering from his wounds, Prophet Jesus left the sepulcher on a Sunday, he then left Israel and headed for the East, where the Ten (10) Lost Tribes and settled. He died at the age of 120, in Srinager, Kashmir, where his Tomb, the Rauzabal Mausoleum is located.

My dear readers, the information that is contained therein , is not in any way meant to condemn, critize or ostracize anyone or any Christian Sect. What this complilation is about, is to actually comment and compliment those who follow the teaching of the Israel Rabbi, Prophet Jesus (Issa), (May God be pleased with him).

To my Christian friends, the following should be noted:

1. "As the cloud is consumed and vanishet away; so he that goeth down to the grave shall come up no more." (Job 07:09-10)

2. "And he said, While the child was yet alive, I fasted and wept: for I said, |Who Can tell whether God will be gracious to me, that the child may live?

But now he is dead, wherefore should I fast? Can I bring him back again? I shall go to him, but he shall not return to me. "(2 Samuel 12:22-23)

3. "And as it is appointed unto men once to die, but after this the judgment." (Epistle to the Hebrews 09:27).

And finally to my Muslim brothers and sisters. Our Holy Prophet Muhammed (s.a.w.s.), settled this controversy; once and for all by saying:

1. "If Moses and Jesus had been alive they would have no choice but to follow me." Tirmazi of Ibn Kathir – Vol.2 pg. 248; also Yawakat wal Jawahir pt.2 pg. 24.

2. "Verily Jesus son of Mary lived for 120 years and I Muhammed see myself as only entering upon the beginning of the sixties. "Kanz-al-Ummâl Pt 6 pg.120.

3. It is recorded in Hadith Bukhari Pt.2 Ch. Al Isra:

"During the Mi'râj (ascension) the prophet saw Jesus and John in the second heaven. "we must, therefore, naturally conclude that either both men are dead or both are physically alive in heaven.

Prophet Muhammed (s.a.w.s.), is reported to have said, the following:

A) " I have several names. I am Muhammed. I am Ahmad. I am Al Aqib (the one who comes last) after whom there is no prophet." Bukhari: Kittab-al-Munuaqib 64:48

B) "Messengership and Prophethood have been cut off. There will be no messenger or prophet after me." Tirmazi.

C) "I am Akhir (last) of the prophets and you are the last of the communities"- Ibn Maja.

D) "The Messenger of Allah said to Ali: you stand to me in the same relation as Aaron stood to Moses except that there is no prophet after me"

Bukhari; Kittab-al-Munaqib-Ali, Muslim and Mishkat-al-Masabih

E) "I am the first prophet in creation but the last in advent.
   "Mishkat-al-Masabih.

And to conclude, the Holy Prophet Muhammed (s.a.w.s.), on the Day of Resurrection will say:

"My Lord, surely my people treat this Qur'an as a forsaken thing."
--- Holy Qur'an 25:30.

PREFACE

The history of the Jews in the Holy Land of Israel, better known as Bait ul-Muquddas, begins with the ancient Israelites, also known Hebrews, who had settled on the ancient lands of Israel. Before the great patriarch (Prophet Abraham), emerged, many other great prophets came before him. Their names are:

Adam, Enoch, Noah, Hud, Salih, Luqman and Dhu-l-Qarnain.

Enter the great Patriarch himself, Prophet Abraham, who throughout his second son Issac and his son Jacob, the Jews originated from. Both Issac and Jacob (according to Islam), were prophets of Allah. In the Holy Qur'an (03:93), Jacob is mentioned by the name Israel.

Jacob was the father of twelve (12) sons, their names being:

1. Reuben, 2. Simeon   3. Levi 4. Judah   5. Issachar
6. Zebulen

7. Joseph   8. Benjamin   9. Dan   10. Naphtali   11. Gad
12. Asher.

Jacob's seventh (7th) son, Joseph, also became a prophet of God. The whole of Chapter 12 of the Holy Qur'an is devoted to the life story of Joseph. The Chapter is simply entitled, Joseph. In the historical account of Joseph's prophethood, there was a draught, we're are told that Joseph, his brothers and their father, eventually settled in Goshen, near the Egypt border; the Israelites were later enslaved by the Egyptians.

Enter the Prophet Moses, Two (2) religious texts has to be mentioned here. The Bible tells us in Deuteronomy 18:15, 18;viz:

"The Lord thy God will rise up unto thee a prophet from the midst of thee, of thy brethren, like unto me; unto him ye shall hearken….

I will rise them up a prophet from among their brethren like unto thee, and will put My words in his mouth."

The Holy Qur'an tells us in Chapter 73:15, the following:

"Surely We have sent to you a Messenger, a witness against you, as We Sent a messenger to Pharaoh."

The individual spoken of, in the two (2), above religious quotations is Islam's Holy Prophet Muhammed (u.w.b.p.).

After being told by Pharaoh, to leave Egypt with his people, Moses, with the guidance of Allah, crosses the Red Sea, he retires for forty days to receive the Law, and sometime there after, the Torah.

Whilst Moses was atop a mountain, the Israelites were simultaneously committing sin, with the worship of an idol (a calf). The brother of the prophet, Aaron, had warned them of committing sin, but they would not listen to him. When his people are commanded to slaughter a cow, the act of quibbling takes place. The other is eventually carried out. A request is made to march onto the Holy Land, the Israelites refuse. They would however wander in the wilderness for forty years.

Before going any further, the predecessors of Prophet Moses wee:

Lot, Ishmael (brother of Issac) and Shu'aib (Jethro).

After the forty years of Wondering in the wilderness, the Israelites returned to the region of Canaan, which was conquered under the command of Prophet Joshua, who divided the region of Gilead amongst the twelve tribes. For a period of time, the united twelve tribes were lead by a series of rulers known as Judges.

After this period, an Israelite monarchy was established under King Saul and continued under King David, who would later conquer Jerusalem and making it his capital. Before becoming King, David would slew the giant called Goliath. (see 1 Samuel 17 and The Holy Qur'an 02:251).

David was not only a king, he was a prophet as well. The heir to David's Kingdom, Solomon, was also a prophet. (see Holy Qur'an 27:16).

When Solomon came to the throne, he widened his kingdom by conquests. My dear readers, I guess you'll have heard of the Queen of Sheba, but did you know of the following;

"It was said to her: Enter the palace. But when she saw it she deemed it to be a great expanse of water, and prepared herself to meet the difficulty. He said: Surely it is a palace made smooth with glass. She said: My Lord, surely I have wronged myself, and I submit with Solomon to Allah, the Lord of the Worlds." (Holy Qur'an 27:44).

At this juncture, the following Prophets of Allah, should be mentioned, they are: Job, Elias, Elisha, Ezekiel and Samuel.

After Solomon's reign, the nation was split into two (2) Kingdoms, the northern kingdom retaining the name Israel, consisting of ten (10) tribes (nine tribes and two divisions of Manasseh), and the southern kingdom of Judah, Simeon and Benjamin.

Israel was conquered by Assyrian ruler Shalmanesar V, in the 8th Century BCE. This is where the dispersion of the Ten (10) Tribes of Israel begins. (see Chapter 06-Migration to the Eastern Countries). The kingdom of Judah was conquered by a Babylonian army in the early 6th Century BCE, the Judahite elite, was exiled to Babylon. After the subsequent conquest of Babylon by the Persians, some of the exiles returned to their homeland, led by the Prophets Ezra and Nehemiah, only to find the Temple destroyed. The second (2nd) Temple was completed under the leadership of the Prophets Haggai, Zachariah and Malachi.

After the death of the three (3) aforementioned prophets, Israel, was still under the control of the Persians. After, Alexander the Great defeated the Persians, and sometime after his demise, there was division within Alexander's Kingdom and amongst his generals; this led to the formation of the Seleucid Kingdom. However things began heading down hill, and a deterioration of religions between Hellenized Jews Religious Jews led the Seleucid King, Antiochus IV, to impose decrees, banning certain Jewish religious rites and traditions.

Consequently, the orthodox Jews revolted under the leadership of the Hasmonean family, also known as the Maccabees. This revolt eventually led to the formation of an independent Jewish Kingdom, known as the Hasmonean Dynasty, which lasted from 165 BCE to 63 BCE. The Maccabees purified the Jewish Temple in Jerusalem, an event that is celebrated to this day on Chanukkah. The Hasmonean Dynasty eventually disintegrated as a result of civil war between siblings; Salome Alexander, Hyracanus II and Aristobulas II.

The Israelites didn't want an absolute monarchy, rather they wanted to be governed by theocratic clergy. They made representation to the Romans for assistance. The Roman campaign of conquest and annexation, led by Pompey, happened in the year of 63 BCE. My dear readers, this is where our historic journey, down the halls of history begins. A journey of knowing and understanding, who Jesus Christ, son of Mary, was, and who he eventually turned out to be … A great Mortal!

CHAPTER 01

The Pious Family Of Amran

In Islam though, the lives of Jesus Christ and his Mother Mary, hold special regard. All Muslims regard Jesus Christ as a righteous Prophet of Allah. His Mother, also a righteous servant of Allah and one (1) of the four (4) perfect and righteous women of Human Creation.

This Chapter deals with the Unknown True Facts, of Mother Mary, her parents, and her initiation into the services of the Temple.

The year of 63 B.C. The Romans conquer a small country on the edge of its empire, that country being known as Palestine.

Our historical account begins in the village of Nazareth, which was part of its empire, that country being in the village of Nazareth, which was part of the town of Galilee. In this village or community, their existed a family whose lineage began with Amran, the father of Moses and Aaron.

It should be noted that the population of Galilee, at this time was mixed. This province counted among its inhabitants the Jews, Phoenicians, Syrians, Arabs and even Greeks.

A mystical Christian Gospel tells us the following:

The blessed and ever glorious Virgin Mary, sprung from the royal race and family of David, was born in the city of Nazareth, and educated at Jerusalem, in the temple of the Lord.

1. Her father's name was Joachim, and Mother's Anna. The family of her father was of Galilee and the city of Nazareth. The family of her mother was of Bethlehem.

1

2. Their lives were plain and right in the sight of the Lord, pious and faultless before men; for they divided all their substance into three parts;

3. One of which they devoted to the temple and officers of the temple; another they distributed among strangers, and persons in poor circumstances; and the third they reserved for themselves and the uses of their own family.

4. In this manner they lived for about twenty years chastely, in the favor of God, and esteem of men, without any children.

5. But they vowed, if God should favour them with any issue, they would devote it to the service of the Lord; on which account they went at every feast in the year to the temple of the Lord.

6. And it came to pass, that when the feast of the dedication drew near, Joachim, with some others of his tribe, when up to Jerusalem, and at the time, Isachar was high-priest;

7. Who, when he saw Joachim along with the rest of his neighbours, bringing his offerings, despised both him and his offerings, and asked him,

8. Why he, who had no children, would presume to appear among those who had? Adding, that his offerings could never be acceptable to God, who was judged by him unworthy to have children; the Scripture having said, Cursed is everyone who shall not beget a male in Israel.

9. He further said, that he ought first to be free from that curse by begetting some issue, and then come with his offerings into the presence of God.

10. But Joachim being much confounded with the shame of such reproach, retired to the shepherds who were with the cattle in their pastures;

11. For he was not inclined to return home, lest his neighbours, who were present and heard all this from the high-priest, should publicly reproach him in the same manner.1

An angle of the Lord (quite possibly, Angel Gabriel) appeared before Joachim and said:

12. Be not afraid, Joachim, nor troubled at the sight of me, for I am an angel of the Lord sent by him to you, that I might inform you hat your prayers are heard, and your alms ascended in the sight of God.

13. For he hath surely seen your shame, and heard you unjustly reproached for not having children: for God is the avenger of sin, and not of nature;

14. And so when he shuts the womb of any person, he does it for this reason, that he may in am more wonderful manner again open it, and that which is born appear to be not the product of lust, but the gift of God.

15. For the first mother of your nation, Sarah, was she not barren even till her eightieth year: and yet even in the end of her old age brought forth Isaac, in whom the promise was made of a blessing to all nations.

16. Rachel, also, so much in favour with God, and beloved so much by holy Jacob, continued barren for a long time, yet afterwards was the mother of Joseph, who was not only governor of Egypt, but delivered many nations from perishing with hunger.

17. Who among the judges was more valiant then Sampson, or more holy than Samuel? And yet both their mothers were barren.

18. But if reason will not conceive you of the truth of my words, that there are frequent conceptions in advanced years, and that those who were barren have brought forth to their great surprise; therefore Anna your wife shall bring you a daughter, and you shall call her name Mary;

19. She shall, according to your vow, be devoted to the Lord from her infancy, and be filled with the Holy Ghost from her mother's womb;

20. She shall neither eat nor drink anything which is unclean, nor shall her conversation be without among the common people, but in the temple of the Lord; that so she may not fall under any slander or suspicion of what is bad.

21. So in the process of her years, as she shall be in a miraculous manner born of one that was barren, so she shall, while yet a virgin, in a way unparalleled, bring forth the Son of the Most High God, who shall, be called Jesus, and, according to the signification of his name, be the Saviour of all nations.

22. And this shall be a sign to you of the things which I declare, namely, when you come to the golden gate of Jerusalem, you shall there meet your wife Anna, who being very much troubled that you returned no sooner, shall then rejoice to see you.

23. When the angle had said this, he departed from him.2

The Angel then appeared before Anna, his wife, saying:
Fear not, neither that which you see is a spirit, he continued thus:

1. For I am that angle who hath offered up your prayers and alms before God, and am now sent to you, that a daughter will be born unto you, who shall be called Mary and shall be blessed above all women.

2. She shall be, immediately upon her birth, full of grace of the Lord, and shall continue during the three years of her weaning in her father's house, and afterwards, being devoted to the service of the Lord, shall not depart from the temple, till she arrive to years of discretion.

3. In a word, she shall there serve the Lord night and day in fasting and prayer, shall abstain from every unclean thing, and never know any man;

4. But, being an unparalleled instance without any pollution or defilement, and a virgin not knowing any man, shall ring forth a son, and a main shall bring forth the Lord, who both by his grace and name and works, shall be the Saviour of the world.

5. Arise therefore, and go up to Jerusalem, and when you shall come to that which is called the golden gate (because it is gilt with gold), as a sign of what I have told you, you shall

meet your husband, for whose safety you have been so much concerned.

6. When therefore you find these things thus accomplished, believe that all the rest which I have told you, shall also undoubtedly be accomplished.

7. According therefore to the command of the angle, both of them left the places where they were, and when they came to the place specified in the angles prediction, they met each other.

8. Then, rejoicing at each other's vision, and being fully satisfied in the promise of a child, they gave due thanks to the Lord, who exalts the humble.

9. After having praised the Lord, they returned home, and lived in a cheerful and assured expectation of the promise of God.

10. So Anna conceived, and brought forth a daughter, and, according to the angel's command, the parents did call name Mary. 3

The holy Qur'an tells us the following:

"When a woman of Amram said: My Lord, I vow to thee what is in my womb, to be devoted (to Thy service), so accept (it) from me; surely Thou, only Thou, art Hearing, the Knowing.

So when she brought it forth she said: My Lord, I have brought it forth a female-and Allah knew best what she brought forth-and the male is not like the female, and I have named it Mary, and I commend her and her offspring into Thy protection from the accursed devil." 4

AND when three years were expired, and the time of her weaning complete, they brought the Virgin to the temple of the Lord with offerings.

1. And there were about temple, according to the fifteen Psalm of degrees, fifteen stairs to ascend.

2. For the temple being built in a mountain, the alter of burnt-offering, which was without, could not be come near but by stairs;

3. The parents of the blessed Virgin and infant Mary put her upon one these stairs;

4. But while they were putting off their clothes, in which they had travelled, and according to custom putting on some that were more neat and clean.

5. In the mean time the Virgin of the Lord in such a manner went up all the stairs one after another, without the help of any to lead her or lift her, that any one would have judged from hence, that he as of perfect age.

6. Thus the Lord did, in the infancy of his Virgin, work this extraordinary work, and evidence by this miracle how great she was like to be hereafter.

7. But the parents having offered up their sacrifice, according to the custom of the law, and perfected their vow, left the Virgin with other virgins in the apartments of the temple, who were to be brought up there, and they returned home. 5

CHAPTER 02

The Virgin Mary And Her Family

Mary, daughter of Joachim and Anna, arrived at womanhood, when she was fourteen (14) years old. As a result, she had to eventually leave eh Temple because of her age.

"No exception was made on her account to the rule which forbade all full grown woman to be seen within the walls of the Holy Temple. The high priest took counsel, as to what course they should adopt in order that she (Mary), should not defile the Lord's Temple."

One (1) day, whilst she prayed and before she left the Temple, an angle appeared before her:

She said: I flee for refuge from thee to Beneficent, if thou art one guarding against evil.

He said: I am only bearer of a message of thy Lord: That I will give thee a pure boy.

She Said: How can I have a son and no mortal has yet touch me, nor have I been unchaste?

He said: So (it will be). Thy Lord says: It is easy to me; and that We may make him a sign to men and a mercy from Us. And it is a matter decreed. 1

In another religious text, we're told the following:

1. Hail, Mary! Virgin of the Lord most acceptable! O Virgin full of grace! The Lord is with you. You are blessed above all women, and you are blessed above all men, that have been hitherto born.

2. But the Virgin, who had before been well acquainted with the countenances of angels, and to whom such light form heaven was no uncommon thing,

3. Was neither terrified with the vision of the angle, nor astonished at the greatness of the light, but only troubled about the angel's words,

4. And began to consider what so extraordinary a salutation should mean, what it did protend, or what sort of end it would have.

5. To this thought the angle, divinely inspired, replies;

6. Fear not, Mary, as though I intended anything inconsistent with your chastity in his salutation:

7. For you have found favour with the Lord, because you made virginity your choice.

8. Therefore while you are a Virgin, you shall conceive without sin, and bring forth a son.

9. He shall be great, because he shall reign from sea to sea, and from the rivers even to the ends of the earth?

10. And he shall be called the Son of the Highest; for he who is born in a mean state on earth, reigns in an exalted one in heaven.

11. And the Lord shall give him the throne of his father David, and he shall reign over the house of Jacob for ever, and of his kingdom there shall be no end

12. For he King of Kings, and Lord of Lords, and his throne is forever and ever.

13. To this discourse of the angle the Virgin replied, not, as though she were unbelieving, but willing to know the manner of it.

14. She said, How can that be? For seeing, according to my vow, I have never known any man, how can I bear a child without the addition of a man's seed.

15. To this the angle replied and said, Think not, Mary, that you shall conceive in the ordinary way. 2

In another Chapter, it goes on to state the following:

1. For she every day had the conversation of angels, and every day received visitors from God, which preserved her from all sorts of evil, and ca used her to abound with all good things;

.

It goes on to state the following:

1. At the time the high-priest made a public order, That all the Virgins who had public settlements in the temple, and were come to this age, should return home, and, as they were now of a proper maturity, should, according to the custom of their country, endeavor to be married.

2. To which command, all the other virgins readily yielded obedience, Mary the Virgin of the Lord alone answered, that she could not comply with it,

3. Assisting these reasons, that both she and her parents had devoted her to the service of the Lord; and besides she had vow virginity to the Lord which vow she was resolved never to break through by lying with a man.

4. The high-priest being hereby brought into a difficulty,

5. Seeing he durst neither on the one hand dissolve the vow, and disobey the Scripture, which says, Vow and pay,

6. Nor on the other hand introduce a custom, to which the people were strangers, commanded,

7. That at the approaching feast all the principal persons both of Jerusalem and the neighbouring places should meet together, that he might have their advice, how he had best proceed in so difficult a case.

8. When they were accordingly met, they unanimously agreed to seek the Lord, and ask counsel from him on this matter.

9. And when they were all engaged in prayer, the high-priest according to the usual way, went to consult God.

10. And immediately there was a voice from the ark, and mercy seat, which all present heard, that it must be enquired or sought out by a prophecy of Isaiah, to whom the Virgin should be given and be betrothed;

11. For Isaiah saith, there shall come forth a rod out of the stem of Jesse, and a flower shall spring out of its root,

12. And the Spirit of the Lord shall rest upon him, the Spirit of Wisdom and Understanding, the Spirit of Counsel and Might, the Spirit of Knowledge and Piety, and the Spirit of the fear of the Lord shall fill him.

13. Then, according to this prophecy, he appointed, that all men of the house and family of David, who were marriageable, and not married should bring their several rods to the altar,

14. And out of whatsoever person's rod after it was brought, a flower should bud forth, and on the top of it the Spirit of the Lord should sit in the appearance of a dove, he should be the man to whom the Virgin should be given and be betrothed.
4

The Holy Qur'an states the following:

'This is of the tidings of things unseen which We reveal to thee. And thou wast not with them when they cast their pens (to decide) which of them should have Mary in his charge, and thou wast not with time when they contended one with another.' 5

Mary's betrothed spouse, is mentioned thus:

AMONG the rest there was a man named Joseph of the house and family of David, and a person very far advanced in years, who kept back his rod, when every one besides presented his.

1. So that when nothing appeared agreeable to the heavenly voice, the high-priest judged it proper o consult God again.

2. Who answered that he whom the Virgin was to be betrothed was the only person of those who were brought together, who had not brought his rod.

3. Joseph therefore was betrayed.

4. For, when he did not bring his rod, and a dove coming form Heaven pitched upon the top of it, every one plainly saw, that the Virgin was to be betrothed to him.

5. Accordingly, the usual ceremonies of betrothing being over, he returned to his won city of Bethlehem, to set his house in order, and make the needful provisions for the marriage.

6. But the Virgin of the Lord, Mary, with seven other virgins of the same age, who had been weaned at the same time, and who had been appointed to attend her by the priest, returned to her parents' house in Galilee. 6

Between the betrothal ceremony and the marriage of Joseph and the follow took place:

And when the angles said: O Mary, surely Allah has chosen thee and purified thee and chosen thee above all women of the world.

O Mary, be obedient to thy Lord and humble thyself and bow down with those who bow.

This is of tidings of things unseen which We reveal to thee. And thou wast not with them when they cast their pens (to decide) which of them should have Mary in his charge, and thou wast not with them when they contended one with another.

When the angles said: O Mary, surely Allah gives thee good news with a word from Him (of one) whose name is Messiah, Jesus, son of Mary, worthy of regard in this world and the Hereafter, and of those who are drawn nigh (to Allah),

And he will speak to the people when in the cradle and when of old age, and (he will be) one of the good ones.

She said: My Lord, how can I have a son and man has not yet touched me? He said: Even so;

Allah creates what He pleases. When He decrees a matter, He only says to it, Be, and it is. 7

Sometimes thereafter, the marriage ceremony takes place and consummation takes place. When it was the period in time, for delivering her child the Holy Qur'an tells us the following

And mention Mary in the Book. When she drew aside from her family to an eastern place; So she screened herself from them. Then We sent her to Our spirit and it appeared to her as a well-made man. She said: I flee for refuge from thee to the Beneficent, if thou art one guarding against evil.

He said: I am only bearer of a message of thy Lord: That I will give thee a pure boy. She said: How can I have a son and no mortal has yet touched me, nor have I been unchaste? He said: So (it will be). Thy Lord says: It is easy to Me; and that We may make him a sign to men and a mercy from Us. And it is a matter decreed. Then she conceived him and withdrew with him to a remote place. And the throes of childbirth drove her to the trunk of a palm-tree, I will drop on thee fresh ripe dates. So eat and drink and cool the eye. Then if thou seest any mortal, say: Surely I have vowed a fast to the Beneficent, so I will not speak to any man today. 8

When the child was born, his name should have been and was in fact Joshua (Aramaic: Jesu; Arabic: Isa) which in Greek is Jesus. Jesus is also referred to in the Gospels as Christ-the Annointed; Messiah-the Wanderer; and Nazarene-the Warner. Joshua or Jeus, Isa or Jesus was his name (Yuz-Asaph-to the Lost Tribes of Israel\); Christ his designation, Messiah his descriptive rank and Nazarene his significant title as a prophet of God.

From this stage, Mary is relegated to the position of a forlorn mother, though she now and again appears, this according to the Aocryphal Gospels.

In the Aquarian Gospel of Jesus, the Christ; Chapter 03 Verse 19, the following is mentioned:

'According to the the custom of the Jews, the child was circumcised; and when they asked, What will you call the child?

The mother said, his name is Jesus (Issa).' (As mentioned aboce).

At this juncture, the following should be mentioned:

The temperature in the area of Bethlehem in December averages around 44 degrees Fahrenheit (7 degrees Celsius), but can drop to well below freezing, especially at night. Describing the weather there, a Senior Israeli weather personnel, noted in a 1990 press release that the area has three months of frost: December with 29 °F. (-6 °C); January with 30°F. (-1°C) and in February with 32°C (0°C.). Snow is common for two or three days in Jerusalem and Bethlehem in December and January. These were the winter months for increased precipitation in Jesus' time, when the roads became practically unusable and people stayed mostly indoors. At the time of Jesus' birth, the shepherds tend their flocks in the fields at night.

A common practice of shepherds was keeping their flocks in the field from April to October, but the cold and rainy winter months they took their flocks back home and sheltered them.

Two (2) facts should be mentioned here; one (1), the Immaculate Conception is actually a metaphor, for when Prophet Jesus was born.

The following biblical excerpts, speaks for themselves, thus:

The Gospel of Matthew Chapter 01 Verse 16 states:

"And Jacob begat Joseph Husband of Mary, of whom was born Jesus, who is called the Christ."

And again,

"Jesus is from the seed of David according to the flesh. "Romans 1:23.

See also Acts 13:22-23 and Galatians 04:04.

The verses are very plain indeed, in that Jesus had to have a natural human genealogy, in order to trace his lineage to David. If his birth were unnatural, that is to say born of Immaculate Conception, then these facts are null and void.

The Gospel of John says:

"And they said, Is not this Joseph's son?" Chapter 04 Verse 22

The Gospel of Mark says:

"Is not this the carpenter, the son of Mary, the brother of James and Joses and of Juda and Simon? And are not his sisters here with us>

-Ch. 06 Verse 03

Jesus and Thomas were twin brothers (born together). In fact, Thomas means twin. Now, how could one be born of Immaculate Conception and the other of a common father, Joseph?

Islam's Holy Prophet Muhammed (u.w.b.p.), once said, during the Najran discussions: "Don't you know that no child is born but has the likeness of his father in form and appearance? They (the Christian Elders of Najran) replied, Yes, we know."

The other interesting fact, in our historic quest of knowing a young Jesus Christ, is getting to know his biological father-Joseph the Carpenter.

Dr. Barbara Thiering, in her book, Jesus-The Man; states on page 392 of her book the following:

"Joseph, son of Jacob-Heli, born 44 B.C. He was given the title 'Joseph' as crown prince to 'Jacob'.

In 8 B.C., he was 36, and due to marry in September of that year. His son, Jesus, was conceived in June, after the final betrothal ceremony but before the wedding. Having a liberal outlook, he choose to continue with the marriage, but when he was under a high priest holding the doctrine of the Hebrews he had to accept James, his next son, was heir.

At the political crisis brought about by the Roman domination, he joined with moderate nationalists, allying with Theudas.

He was the 'star' (of David) to Theudas 'Secptre.'

Joseph became the potential David on the death of Jacob-Heli in A.D. 17.

He died in A.D. 23."

Enter Herod, the Great. Born 74B.C. and died around the year of 4.A.D. Herod's reign began in 39 B.C. and ended in the said year of 4A.D. Before Herod died, three (3) magians from beyond the Euphrates river, were observing the stars of heaven (they were Persians Astrlogers), one night: and after conversing with one and another, off what they found, decided to hasten to the West, in search of the new born king, who was foretold to be born in the holy land of Palestine. Their search brought them to Judaea and then onto Jerusalem and they enquired:

"Where should the Christ be born?" They answered:

"The prophets long ago foretold that one would come to rule the tribes of Israel; that this Messiah would be born in Bethlehem.

They also said. The Prophet Micah wrote,

O Bethlehem Judea, a little place among the Judean hills, yet out of you will come forth to rule my people, Israel; yea, one who lived in olden times, in very ancient days." 9

Herod accordingly called back in magi (they were sent out of Herod's court, so-that, Herod could seed advise), and told them concerning their prophesy, he told them:

"Go to Bethlehem and search out with all diligence concerning the child; and when you have found him, come and tell it to me, because I also would gladly come and worship him. And this he spoke deceitfully." 10

The Infant Jesus, was not born in a manger nor a cave.

Bethlehem, it seems may have been a town. That had large followers of the Nazarean Essence, because on the outskirts of this town, is where tie Infant Jesus-may have been born. (see Holy Qur'an Ch. 19 Verses 23-26).

The Three Magians, had in fact met mother, son and quite possible, the Infant's father at the Temple in Bethlehem.

They then presented onto the infant gifts of gold, frankincense and myrrh.

Before the Magians met the family, an incident took place:

"And in the temple was a widow, four and eighty years of age, and she departed not, but night and day she worshipped God. And when she saw the infant Jesus she exclaimed, Behold Immanuel! Behold the signet cross of the Messiah on his brow! And then the woman knelt to worship him, as God with us, Immanuel; but one, a master, clothed in white, appeared and said,

Good woman, stay; take heed to what you do; you may not worship man; this is idolatry. This child is man, the son of man, and worthy of all praise. You shall adore and worship God; him only shall you serve. The woman rose and bowed her head in thankfulness and worshipped God.

And Mary took the infant Jesus and returned to Bethlehem." 11

The Three Magians, who could read the hearts of men, read the wickedness of Herod's heart and they knew he had one thing on his mind, Herod had silently sworn to kill the new born king.

"And so they told the secrets to the parents of the child, and bid them flee beyond the reach of harm. And then the priests (Magian's) went on their homeward way; they went not through Jerusalem. And Joseph took the infant Jesus and his mother in the night and fled to Egypt land, and with Elihu and Salome in ancient Zoan they abode." 12

The only Savior of the world is love, and Jesus, son of Mary, comes to manifest that love to men. Now, love cannot manifest until its way has been prepared, and naught can rend the rocks and bring down lofty hills and fill the valleys up, and thus prepare the way, but purity.

But purity in life, men do not comprehend but little of the works shall pave the way for love; but not a word is lost, for in the Book of God's Remembrance a registry is made of every thought, and word and deed;

And when the world is ready to receive, lo, God will send a messenger to open up the book, and copy from its sacred pages all the messages of Purity and Love. Then every man on earth will read the words of life in language of his native land, and men will see the light, walk in the light and be the light.

And man will again, be at one with God." 13

Master teacher, Brother Elihu's lesson to both Mary and Elizabeth were thus: 14

1.   The Unity of Life: 'No man lives unto himself; for every living thing is bound by cords to every other living thing. Bless are the pure in heart; for they will love and not demand love in return.

2.   The Two Selfs: The higher self is human spirit clothed with soul, made in the from of God. The lower self, the carnal self, the body of desires, is a reflection of the higher self, distorted by the murky enters of the flesh. And et cetera...........

3.   The Devil.

4.   Love-the savior of men.

5.   The David of the Light.

6.   Goliath of the dark.

Master teacher, Sister Salome's lessons were as follows: 15

1.   The Man and the Woman: In all the ways of life the man and woman should walk hand in hand; the one without the other is but half; each has a work to do. And et cetera............

2.   Philosophy of Human moods: Today one hates and scorns and envies and is jealous of the child he loves; tomorrow he has risen above his carnal self, and breathes forth gladness and good will. And et cetera..........

3.   Theology.

Master teacher, Brother Elihu's Second lessons were as follows:

1.   The Vedic Religion of India: Their laws were just; they lived in peace; with carnal aims arose, who changed the laws to suit the carnal mind; bound heavy burdens on the poor, and scorned the rules of right; and so the Brahms became corrupt. And et cetera...

2.   The Life of Abraham.

3.   Books of the Jewish Faith.

4.   The Persian Religion and its Spiritual head, named Zarathustra.

Master teacher, Brother Elihu's Third Lesson was as follows: 17

1. Buddhism and the precepts of Buddha: Hate is a cruel word. If men hate you regard it not; and you can turn the hate of men to love and mercy and goodwill, and cercy is large as all the heavens. And et cetera...........

2. The Mysteries of Egypt: The land of Egypt is the land of secret things.

Master teacher, Sister Salome's second lesson and Final lesson of Brother Elihu's is as follows:

The Sister said: Behold the sun! It manifests the power of God who speaks to us through the sun and moon and the stars; Throughout mountain, hill and vale; through flower, and plant and tree. And et cetera.........

Master teacher, Brother Elihu spoke for the last time; he said: 18

Our words are said; you need not tarry longer here; the call has come, the way is clear, you may return unto your native land. A mighty work is given unto you, to do, you shall direct the minds that will direct the world. And et cetera........

All the foregoing lessons, lasted for almost three (3) years. After which both families; Joseph, Mary and Jesus along with Elisabeth and her son John returned home to Israel, where Herod's son-Archelaus, reigned form Jerusalem.

At the home of Joseph, which was in the Nazareth town, it was here that Lady Mary taught her son the lessons of Master teacher's Elinha and Salome.

"and Jesus greatly loved the Vedic hymns and the Avesta; but more than all he loved to read the Psalms of David and the pungent words of Solomon.

The Jewish books of prophecy were his delight; and when he reached his seventh year he needed not the books to read, for he had fixed in memory every word" 19

His Grandparents, Joachim and Hanna made a feast in honour of their grand child and all of heir near of kin were their guests.

Joachim said: "My son, today you pass the seventh milestone of your way of life, for you are seven years of age, and we will give to you, as a remembrance delight.

And Jesus said, I do not want a gift, for I am satisfied. If I could make a multitude of children glad upon this day, I would be greatly pleased/

Now, there are many hungry boys and girls in Nazareth who would be pleased to eat with us this feast and share with us the pleasure of this day.

The richest gift that you can give me is your permission to go out and find these needy ones and bring them here that they may feast with us.

Joachim said, 'Tis well; go out and find the needy boys and girls and bring them here; we will prepare enough for all. And Jesus did not wait; he ran and entered every dingy, hut and cabin of the town, he didn't waste his words, he told his mission everywhere.

And in a little time, one hundred and sixty (160) happy, ragged boys and girls were following him up Marmion Way (an avenue or a street).

The guests made way, the banquet hall was filled with Jesus' guests, and Jesus and his mother helped to serve. And there was food enough or all, and all were glad, and so the birthday gift Jesus was a crown of righteousness." 20

Before the Feast of Righteousness, something strange took place.

A young Jesus, stood before his guests and said the following:

"I had a dream, and I stood before a sea, upon a sandy beach. The waves upon the sea were high; a storm was raging on the deep. Someone above gave me a wand. I took the wand and touched the sand, and every grain of sand became a living thing; the beach was all a mass of beauty and of song. I touched the waters at my feet, and they were changed to trees, and flowers and singing birds, and everything was praising God.

And someone spoke, I did not see the one who spoke, I heard the voice, which said, THERE IS NO DEATH.

His Grandmother, Hanna, loved her grandchild, she laid her hand of Jesus' head and said: I saw you beside the sea, I saw you touch the sand and waves I saw them turn to living things and I knew the meaning of the dream.

The sea of life rolls high, the storms are great. The multitude of men are idle, listless, waiting, like dead sand upon the beach. Your wand is truth. With this you touch the multitudes, and every man becomes a messenger of holy light and life. You touch the waves upon the sea of life, their turmoils cease, the very wind become a song of praise.

There is no death, because the wand of truth can change the driest bones to living things, and bring the loveliest flowers from stagnant ponds, and turn the most discordant notes to harmony and praise." 21

Enter Rabbi Barachia of the synagogue of Nazareth.

The Rabbi was aid to Mary in the teaching of her son. One morning after service in the synagogue, the Rabbi asked Jesus, as he sat in silent thought; Which is the greatest of the Ten Commands that binds them fast and makes them one.

This cord is love, and it belongs to every word of all the Tem Commands.

If one is full of love he can do nothing else than worship God; for God is love.

If one is full of love, he cannot kill, he cannot falsely testify, he cannot covet, can do naught but honor God, and man. If one is full of love he does not need commands of any kind.

Rabbi Barachia said, Your words are seasoned with the salt of wisdom that is from above. Who is the teacher who has opened up this truth to you?

And Jesus said, I do not know that any teacher opened up this truth for me.

It seems to me that truth was never shut, that it was always opened up, for truth is one and it is everywhere. And if we open up the windows of our minds the truth will enter in and make herself at home, for truth can find her way through any crevice, any window, any open door.

The Rabbi said, What hand is strong to open up the windows and the doors for mind, so truth can enter in?

And Jesus said, it seems to me that love, the golden cord that binds the Ten Commands in one, is strong enough to open any human door, so that the truth can enter in and cause the hearth to understand." 22

When Jesus was ten years old, the Jews had a great feat. His parents and many of their kin were in attendance-including himself.

And Jesus watched the butchers slaughter the lamb and birds and burn them on the altar in the name of God. His tender heart was shocked at this display of cruelty, he asked the serving priests:

What is the purpose of this slaughter of the beasts and birds? Why do you burn their flesh before the Lord? The Priest replied,

This is our sacrifice for sin. God has commanded us to do these things, and said that in these sacrifices all our sins are blotted out. And Jesus said,

Will you be kind enough to tell when God proclaimed that sin are blotted out by sacrifice of any kind?

Did not David say that God requires not sacrifice for sin? That it is a sin itself to bring before his face burnt offerings, as offerings for sin? Did not Isaiah say the same? The priest replied,

My child you are besides yourself. Do you know more about the laws of God than all the priests of Israel? This is no place for boys to show their wit.

But Jesus heeded not his taunts; he went to Hillel, chief of the Sanhedrin, and he said to him,

Rabbomi, I would like to talk with you; I am disturbed about the service of the pascal feast. I thought the temple was the house of God, where love and kindness dwell. Do you not hear the bleating of those lambs, the pleading of those doves that men are killing over there? Do you not smell that awful stench that comes form burning flesh? Can men be kind and just, and still be filled with cruelty? A God that takes delight in sacrifice, in blood and burning flesh, is not my Father-God.

But Hillel could not give an answer to the child. His heart was stirred with sympathy. He called the child to him. Laid his hand upon his head and wept. He said, There is a God of love, and you shall come with me; and hand in hand we will go forth and find the God of love. And Jesus said,

Why must we go? I thought that God is everywhere; Can we not purify our hearts and drive out cruelty, and every wicked thought, and make within, a temple where the God of love can dwell?

The master of the great Sanhedrin felt as though he was himself the child, and that before him stood Rabboni, master of the higher law.

He said within himself, This child is surely a prophet sent from God.

Then Hillel sought the parents of the child, and asked that Jesus might abide with them, and learn the precepts of the law, and all the lessons of the temple priests. His parents gave consent, and Jesus did abide with them, and learn the precepts of the law, and all the lessons of the temple in Jerusalem, and Hillel taught him everyday.

And everyday the master learned from Jesus many lessons of the higher life. The child remained with Hillel in the temple for a year, and then returned unto his home in Nazareth, and there he wrought with Joseph (his father), as a carpenter." 23

Issa (Jesus) grew up to be an intelligent child. He was obedient and dutiful to both his parents and was very kind to everyone. Due to his pious upbringing he spoke words of wisdom from his early childhood and whenever he was confronted with difficult and complex questions, his answers were so enlightening and wonderful which were not expected from a child of his age.

According the Gospel of Barnabas it mentioned the following:

Jesus, having come to the age of twelve years, went up with Mary and Joseph to Jerusalem, to worship there according to the law of the Lord written in the book of Moses. When their prayers were ended they departed, having lost Jesus, because they thought that he was returned home with their kinsfolk.

Mary therefore returned with Joseph to Jerusalem, seeking Jesus among kinsfolk and neighbours. The third day they found the child in the temple, in the mist of the doctors, disputing with them concerning the law. And everyone was amazed at his questions and answers, saying: "How can there be such doctrine in him, seeing he is so small and have not learned to read?"

Mary reproved him, saying: 'Son, what has thou done to us?

'Jesus answered: 'Know you not that the service of God ought to come before father and mother?' Jesus then went down with his mother and father to Nazareth, and was subject to them with humility and reverence.

For the next twelve months, a teenaged Jesus lived with his parents in Nazareth, for a small secluded town amongst the hills of Galilee, the land of pastures, olives groves and vineyards.

It should be noted at this juncture that Jesus of Nazareth, was not born on December 25th., as the Roman-Catholic Church would like millions upon millions of its followers and non Catholics to believe.

The concept of the birth of Jesus on the 25th. of December, corresponds to paganism, viz:-

1. ATTIS (the sun-god) is said to be born of the virgin Nana. He was regarded as the Only Begotten Son and Saviour. He was sacrificed and he was resurrected on the 24th of March. His blood was shed in order that the sins of man may be forgiven.

2. ASONIS of TAMMUZ (SYRIA)

He was virgin born and was considered to be the Saviour. He was sacrificed for redemption of mankind. He is referred to in the Bible as Promised Saviour. (Exekiel 8:14)

3. DIONYSIS of BACCHUS

The only begotten son of Jupiter, was born of the virgin Demeter on December 25th. He was Redeemer, Liberator and Saviour.

4. BEL of BAAL

He was the sun-god of Babylon, and answers to all the description of Jesus, as is preached by the Church

5. OSIRIS

He was born on December 29th in Egypt. He preached the gospel of gentleness and peace. He was betrayed by Typhen, slain and dismembered. He was interred but came again to life after remaining in hell for approximately three days and three nights.

6. MITHRA

He was the virgin born sun-god of the Persians. He came into the world as an infant. His first worshippers were shepherds and his birthday was December 25th. His followers practiced baptism, confirmation, Euchariastic supper and partook of the divine nature of Mithra under the species of bread and wind.

7. THE MEXICAN VIRGIN-BORN QUETZALCOALT.

He was just like Jesus in every description, although he is said to have appeared so many hundred years before Jesus.

The Holy Qur'an's commentary by Maulana Muhamad Ali says in note 1539a the following:

"The Qur'an does not accept that Jesus was born on 25th December.

It was the time when fresh ripe dates are found on palm-trees (meaning the period in time in which Jesus was born; he was born somewhere in the middle of the Christian Calendar-between May and August).

A very known Bishop named Bishop Barnes says in the Rise of Christianity;

"There is, moreover, no authority for the belief that December 25th was the actual birthday of Jesus. If we can give any credence to the birth-story of Luke, with the shepherds keeping watch by night in the fields near Bethlehem, the birth of Jesus did not take place in winter, when the night temperature is so low in the hill country of Jedaea that snow is not uncommon.

After such argument our Christmas day seems to have been accepted about A.D. 300" (p.79)."

The Aforementioned facets above speaks for themselves; I need not to say anything more.......

Earlier in this chapter, I mentioned Islam's Holy Prophet Muhammed meeting and receiving a delegation of Christian Elders from Najran. During this discussion, the question of the father of Jesus arose, the Prophet gave a two (2) part answer to the above question, the following is the second (2nd.) part of this answer:

"Don't you know that Jesus was conceived by a woman just as any other woman conceives a child? Then she gives birth to him like every other woman gives birth to a child, he was reared up like other children then he used to eat and drink and answer the call of nature like other human beings? They said, "Yes, we know." Tafsir of Ibn-i-Jarir Tabari Volume 03 Verses 100-101.

My dear readers, how can my Muslim and Christian sisters and brothers, go against such abundance of factual testimonies and still uphold that Prophet Jesus had a fatherless birth?

Since all prophets, including Jesus, were human beings, then the only way out of this is dilemma is to deny he was human and to postulate, that he was divine! The next chapter deals with, the missing years of Jesus Christ.

Author's Note: Earlier in this Chapter, I mentioned about the temperature in the area of Bethlehem and which was from a Senior Israeli Weather Personnel and noted in a 1990 Press Release; that person is Sara Ruhin, and to her, I hope its okay for me in mentioning your name here – Thanks!

CHAPTER 03

The Unknown Years Of Prophet Jesus

This chapter is no heresy and is not fictional; it is based on the evidence that has survived through the centuries. This information is FACTUAL. Many Christians and Islamic Scholars will say things to contradict these facts. They may even go as far in condemning the foregoing information and declare that some unknown writer/author was daydreaming or something of this nature.

Before giving, you my readers, the historical account of Jesus (Issa), journeying to India, the following must be mentioned;

World renown Theologist of the twenty-first (21st.) century, Dr. Zakir Naik, wrote a world famous book entitled; 'Concept of God in Major Religions', in which the following is mentioned:

"Aryan religions are the religions that originated amongst the Aryans, a powerful group of Indo-European speaking people that spread through Iran and Northern India in the first half of eh second Millennium BC (2000 to 1500 BC). The Aryan Religions are further subdivided into Vedic and non-Vedic religions. The Vedic Religion is given the misnomer of Hinduism or Brahminism. The non-Vedic religion Sikhism, Buddhism, Janism etc….. Zoroastrianism is an Aryan, non-Vedic religion, which is not associated with Hinduism. It claims to be a prophetic religion."

The following should also be mentioned. It is taken from, Nicholas Notovitch's book; 'The Unknown Life of Jesus Christ', page 81, it says:

"After the world had appeared by the mere wish of Parp-Brahma, God created men, whom he divided into four (4) classes, according to their colour;

1.	Brahamans – White	2.	Kshatriyas – Red
8.	Vaisyas – Yellow	4.	Soudras – Black.

And the following piece of historical fact, could shed some light, into why young Jesus, would want to visit India, when he was still a teenager. Could it be that India, produced prophets of God Almighty, who came to the Lost Trines of Israel, or those prophets came to India, which was known as Hindustan and the Indus Cush Valley?

In Islam, there are the Hadiths', where the sayings of Prophet Muhammed (r.w.b.p.) are recorded. One such compilation is the Dailami; this book is not generally known to Muslim Scholars. Nevertheless, Prophet Muhammed (u.w.b.p.) says, 'There has been a prophet in India, whose colour was dark and his name was Kahina (Krishna).'

The evidence of Prophet Jesus, visiting the East in his childhood and teenage years can be found in two (2) documents viz; The Unknown Life of Jesus Christ by Nicholas Notovitch and The Aquarian Gospel of Jesus the Christ, of which I have quoted and taken excerpts from.

And now the historical account of Jesus (Issa), journeying to India and surrounding countries, when he was a teenager.

When Issa had attained the age of thirteen years, the epoch when an Israelite should take a wife. The house where his parents earned their living by carrying on a modest trade began to be a p lace of meeting for rich and noble people, desirous of having for a son-in-law the young Issa, who already famous for his edifying discourses in the name of the Almighty.

Then it was that Issa left the parental house in secret and departed from Jerusalem, and with in the company of merchants set out towards India, with the object of perfecting himself in the Divine word and of studying the laws of the great Buddhas.

In the course of his fourteenth year, the young Issa, blessed by God, journeyed beyond India and settled amongst the Aryas in the land beloved of God.

As the fame and reputation of this marvelous child spread throughout the Length of Northern India, and when he crossed the country of he five rivers and Rajputana, the devotees of the pagan diety Janie begged him to stay in their midst (It seems he went their to study their cult).

He then went to Shalabeth (Sri Lanka) and from there to Jaganath (Jaggernauth), in the country of Orissa, where lies the remains of Vyasu-

Krishna (Krishna was a Prophet from amongst the Dravidians) and where the white priests of Brahma give him a joyous welcome.

The white priests of Brahma taught him to read and understand the Vedas, the heal by prayer, to teach and explain the Holy Scripture, to cast out evil spirits from the body of man and give back to him, human semblances

He passed six years at Jagannath, at Rajagriha, at Benaris, and in other holy cities. All loved him for Issa lived inpeace with the Vaisyas and the Soudrad, to whom he taught the Holy Scriptures. But the Brahmans and Kshatriyas told him that the were forbidden by the great Para-Brahma to come near to those whom he had created from his side and feet.

Issa denied the divine origin of the Vedas and the Puranas. For he taught his followers the following:

"A law has already been given to man to guide him in his actions; fear thy God, bend the knee before him only, and bring to him alone the offerings which proceed form thy gains.

Issa denied the Trimurti and the incarnation of Para-Brahma in Vishnu, Siva, and other gods, for he said (also):

'The Eternal Judge, the Eternal Spirit, comprehends, and vivifies all. He alone has willed and created, he alone has willed and created, he alone has existed since all eternity, or on earth. The Great Creator has not shared his power with any living being, still less with inanimate objects, as they have taught you; for he alone possesses omnipotence. He willed it and the world appeared. In a divine thought, he gathered together the waters, separating from them the dry portion of the globe. He is the principle of the mysterious existence of man, in whom he has breathed a part of his Being.

And he has subordinated to man the earth, the waters, the beasts, and all that he has created and that he himself preserves in immutable order, fixing for each thing the length of its duration.

The anger of God will soon be let loose against man; for he has forgotten his Creator, he has filled his temples with abominations, and he worships a crowd of creatures which God has made subordinate to him.

For to do honor to stones and meals, he sacrifices human beings, in whom dwells a part of the spirit for the Most High.

For he humiliates those who work by the sweat of their brow to acquire the favor of an idler seated at his sumptuous board.

Those who deprive their brethren of divine happiness shall be deprived of it themselves. The Brahamans and the Kshatriyas shall become the Sudras, and will the Sudras the Eternal shall dwell everlastingly.

Because in the day of the last judgment the Sudras and the Vaisyas will be forgiven much because of their ignorance, while God, on the contrary, will punish with his wrath those who have arrogated to themselves his rights.

The Vaisyas and the Sudras were filled with great admiration and asked Issa how they should pray so as not to lose their eternal felicity. Worship not the idols, for they hear you not. Listen not to the Vedas, for their truth is counterfeit. Never put yourself in the first place and thou has not and which thou seest belongeth to another." 1

After the discourse, Issa was warnes of the impending danger on his life by the Soudras, he fled in the night from Jagannath, reached the mountains, and established himself at Kapilavastu, Nepal, birthplace of Gautam-Sakyamuni-Buddah. After having perfected himself in the Pali language, the just Issa applied himself to study the sacred writings of the sutras. The Buddhists opened wide the doors of a monastery for him, and he started living amongst the monks. He witnessed their religious rites and participated in their prayers. A time came when he fully understood the words of the Master and began to teach on the same lines. The head Lama declared in a congregation:

'We stand today upon a Crest of time'
Six times ago a master soul was born,
Who gave a glory light to man,
And now a master sage stands here,
This Hebrew prophet is the rising star of wisdom,
He brings to us a knowledge of God;
And all the world will hear his words,
Will heed his words,
And glorify his name.'

Six years after Issa, whom the Buddha elected to spread his holly word, had become a perfect expositor of the sacred writings.

He then left Nepal and the Himalayan mountains, descended into the valley of Rajputana, and went towards the west, preaching to diverse people the supreme perfection of man, in those words:

'He who shall have regained his original purity;
Will die having obtained,

Remission for his sins;
And he will have the right,
To contemplate the majesty of God.
The Eternal Law-giver is one;
There is no other God but him;
He has not shared the world with anyone,
Neither has he informed anyone of his intentions.'
He also taught them:
"Even as a father would act towards his children, so will God judge man after their deaths according to the laws of his mercy.

Never would he so humiliate his child as to transmigrate his soul, as in a purgatory, into the body of an animal."

The words of Issa spread among the pagans in the midst of the countries he traversed, and the inhabitants forsook their idols. In one sojourn, Issa declared: 'If your idols and your animals are powerful and really possessed of supernatural strength, then let them strike me to the earth.'

The priests then answered: "Work then a miracle, and let thy God confound our gods, if they inspire him with contempt."

But Issa then said; "The miracles our God have been worked since the first day when the universe was created; they take place everyday and at every moment. Whosoever seeth them not is deprived of one of the fairest gifts of life."

Seeing the powerlessness of their priest, the pagans had still greater faith in the saying of Issa an fearing the anger of the Divinity, broke their idols to pieces. As for the priest, they fled to escape the vengeance of the populace.

The neighbouring countries resounded with the prophecies of Issa, and when he entered into Persia (on his homeward sojourn), the priests became alarmed and forbade the inhabitants from listening to him. And when they saw all the villagers welcoming him with joy and devoutly accepting his sermons. The priests had him arrested and interrogated thus:

"Of what new God does thou speak of? Are you not aware, unhappy man, that Saint Zoroaster (he was a prophet of God) is the only just one admitted to the privileged of communication with the Supreme Being, 'Who ordered the angles to put down in writing the word of God for the use of his people, laws that were given to Zoroaster in paradise?

'Who then are you to dare to blaspheme our God and to sow doubt in the hearts of believers?'

28

And Issa said unto them: 'It is not of a new God that I speak but of our Heavenly Father, who has existed since all time and who will still be after the end of all things'."

He also told them the following:

'He told them not to worship the sun, for it was part of the cosmos which God has created for humanity. It is God and to God alone, that we owe all that possess in this world. On hearing this, the priests asked him; 'How could a people live according to the rules of justice if it had no preceptors?'

Jesus replied: 'So long as the people had no priests, natural law governed them and they preserved the candour of their souls. He further explained that when their souls were with God, they could commune with the 'Father', without the medium of any idol or animal or the Sun or the fire.........'

After having listened to him, the magi determined to do him no harm. But at night when all the town lay asleep, they took him and placed him out-side of the walls and abandoned him on the high road, in the hope that he would soon become prey to the wild beasts. But protected by the Lord our God, the young prophet continued his way, unmolested.

At this juncture, two(2) things should be noted. One, whilst Issa was in India, near the Ganges, he received unwelcome news of the passing of his father, Joseph-the carpenter, from a caravan, who were returning from the West. Secondly, there are critics, who would declare that : Prophet Jesus never visited India, during those missing years. To those who dare not to accept the facts, read the following from, The Aquarian Gospel of Jesus the Christ, Chapter 27:

Chapter 27

Jesus attends a .feast in Behar. Preaches a revolutionary sermon on human equality. Relates the parable of the broken blades.

1. The fame of Jesus as a teacher spread through all the land, and people came from near and far to hear his words of truth.

2. At Behar, on the sacred river of the Brahms, he taught for many days.

3. And Ach, a wealthy man of Behar, made a feast in honour of his guest, and he invited every one to come.

4. And many came; among them thieves, extortioners, and courtesans. And Jesus sat with them and taught; but they who

followed him were much aggrieved because he sat with thieves and courtesans.

5.   And they upbraided him; they said, Rabboni, master of the wise, this day will be an evil day for you.

6.   The news will spread that you consort with courtesans and thieves, and men will shun you as they shun an asp.

7.   And Jesus answered them and said, A master never screens himself for sake of reputation or of fame.

8.   These are but worthless baubles of the day; they rise and sink, like empty bottles on a stream; they are illusions and will pass away;

9.   They are the indices to what the thoughtless think; they are the noise that people make; and shallow men judge merit by noise.

10. God and all master men judge men by what they are and not by what they seem to be; not by their reputation and their fame.

11. These courtesans and thieves are children of my Father-God; their soul are just as precious in his sight as yours, or of the Brahmic priests.

12. And they are working out the same life sums that you, who pride yourselves on your respectability and moral worth, are working out.

13. And some of them have solved much harder sums than you have solved, you men who look at them with scorn.

14. Yes, they are sinners, and confess their guilt, while you are guilty, but are shrewd enough to have polished coat to cover up your guilt.

15. Suppose you men who scorn these courtesans, these drunkards and these thieves, who know that you are pure in heart and life, that you are better far than they, stand forth that men may know just who you are.

16. The sin lies in the wish, in the desire, not in the act.

17. You covet other people's wealth; you look at charming forms, and deep within your hearts you lust for them.

18. Deceit you practice every day, and wish for gold, for honour and for fame, just for your selfish selves.

19. The man who covets is a thief, and she who lusts is courtesan. You who are none of these speak out.

20. Nobody spoke; the accusers held their peace.

21. And Jesus said, The proof this day is all against those who have accused.

22. The pure in heart do not accuse. The vile in heart who want to cover up their guilt with holy smoke of piety are ever loathing drunkard, thief and courtesan.

23. This loathing and this scorn is mockery, for if the tinselled coat of reputation could be torn away, the loud professor would be found to revel in his lust, deceit and many forms of secret sin.

24. The man who spends his time in pulling other people's weeds can have no time to pull his own, and all the choicest flowers of life will soon be choked and die, and nothing will remain but darnel, thistles, burs.

25. And Jesus spoke a parable: he said, Behold, a farmer had great fields of ripened grain, and when he looked he saw that blades of many stalks of wheat were bent and broken down.

26. And when he sent his reapers forth he said, We will not save the stalks of wheat that have the broken blades.

27. Go forth and cut and burn the stalks with broken blades.

28. And after many days he went to measure up his grain, but not a kernel could be find. And then he called the harvesters and said to them, Where is my grain?

29. They answered him and said, We did according to your word; we gathered up and burned the stalks with broken blades, and not a stalk was left to carry to the barn.

30. And Jesus said, If God saves only those who have no broken blades, who have been perfect in his sight, who will be saved?

31. And the accusers hung their heads in shame; and Jesus went his way.

After visiting many towns and hamlets, thereafter, and in his twenty-ninth year, he crossed the Jordan to his native land. And at once he sought his home in Nazareth.

His mother's heart was filled with joy; she made a feast for him, inviting all her kindred and her friends. But Jesus' brothers were not pleased that such attention should be paid to one they deemed a sheer adventurer, and they were not in to the feast. They laughed their brother's claim to scorn; they called him indolent, ambitious, vain; a worthless fortune hunter; searcher of the world for fame, who, after many years returns to mother's home with neither gold, nor any other wealth.

And Jesus called aside his mother and her sister, Miriam, and told them of his

journey to the East. He told them of the lessons he had learned, and of the works that he had done. To others he told not the story of his life.

The Aquarian Gospel of Jesus, the Christ, also tells us the following (providing that this information is accurate):

After his visit to his home in Nazareth, Issa longed to study with the masters of Greek philosophy in the schools of Greece, for Greek philosophy was full of pungent truth. So he left his home in Nazareth and crossed the Carmel Hills, and at the port, took a snip and soon he was in the Grecian capital. Now the Athenians had heard of him as a teacher and philospher, and they were glad to have him in their company, so that they may hear his words of truth. Now amongst the masters of the Greeks was one Apollo, who was called Defender of the Oracle, and recognized in many lands as a Grecian sage.

Apollo opened up all the doors of Grecian lore and in the Areopages he heard the wisest masters speak. Once in an Amphitheatre, Apollo asked him to speak, and he said:

'Oh Athenian masters! In ages long ago, men, wise in nature's laws sought out and found the place on which your city stands. Full well you know that there are parts of earth where its great beating heart throws heavenward etheric waves that meet the ethers from above: Where spirit-light and understanding, like the stars of night, shine forth of all the parts of earth there is no place more sensitized, more truly spiritblessed, than that where Athens stands.

Yes, all of Greece is blessed. No other land has been the homeland of such mighty men of thought as grace your scrolls of fame.

A host of sturdy giants of philosophy, of poetry, of science, and of art, were born upon the soil of Greece, and rocked to manhood in your cradle of pure thought. I come not here to speak of science, of philosophy, or art; of these you are the world's best masters now.

But all your high accomplishments are but stepping stones to worlds beyond the realm of sense; are but illusive shadows fitting on the walls of time. But I would tell you of a life beyond, within; a real life that cannot pass away.

In science and philosophy there is no power strong enough to fit a soul to recognize itself, or to commune with God. I would not stay the flow of your great streams of thought; but I would turn them to the channels of the soul.

Unaided by the Spirit-breath, the work of intellection tends to solve the problems of the things we see, and nothing more. The senses were ordained to bring into mind mere pictures of the things that pass away; they do not deal with real things, they do not comprehend eternal law. But man has something in his soul, a something that will tear the veil apart that he may see the world of real things.

We call this something, spirit consciousness; it sleeps in every soul, and cannot be awakened till the Holy Breath becomes a welcome guest. This Holy Breath knocks at the door of every soul, but cannot enter in until the will of man throws wide the door.

There is no power in intellect to turn the key; philosophy and science both have toiled to get a glimpse behind the veil; but they have failed. The secret spring that throws ajar the door of the soul is touched by nothing else than purity in life, by prayer and holy thought..

Return, O mystic stream of Grecian thought, and mingle your clear waters with the flood of Spirit-life; and then the spirit consciousness will sleep no more, and man will know, and God will bless. "2.

When Jesus had thus spoken, he stepped aside. The Grecian masters were astonished at the wisdom of his words; they answered not.

Jesus/Issa visit to Greece was a brief one, however it is unclear how many days or weeks he spent in Greece.

But when his sojourn was over he visited Egypt, where he went at once to Zoan, home of Master teachers, Elihu and Salome.

(It should be noted here that it seems that these two master teachers were members of the Egyptian Essenes spiritual community).

It was within this community that Issa underwent training; spiritual training that contained seven(7) degrees-viz:

1. Sincerity   2.   Justice   3.   Faith
    4.   Philanthrophy

2. Heroism   6.   Love Divine   and the seventh, is the degree, that gave him the title that we knows' him as; THE CHRIST-The Anointed.

The next chapter deals with his prophetic Office, as a Messenger of God.

Chapter 04

The Prophet And His Ministry

The Prophet of God, had now matured into a young man. After his alleged sojourn to Greece and back, he sometime thereafter, journeyed to Mount Olive, where the following took place:

Jesus having come to the age of thirty years, as he himself said unto me, went up to Mount Olives with his mother to gather olives. Then at midday as he was praying, when he came to these words: 'Lord, with mercy….,' he was surrounded by an exceeding bright light and by an infinite multitude of angels, who were saying: 'Blessed be God.' The angel Gabriel presented to him as it were a shining mirror, a book, which descended into the heart of Jesus, in which he had knowledge of what hath said and what God willeth insomuch that everything was laid bare and open to him; as he said unto me: 'Believe, Barnabas, that I know every prophet with every prophecy, insomuch that whatever I say the whole bath come forth form that book.'

Jesus, having received this vision, knowing that he was a prophet sent to the house of Israel, revealed all to Mary his mother, telling her that he needs must suffer great persecution for the honour of God, and that he could not any longer abide with her to serve her. Whereupon, having heard this, Mary answered; 'Son ere thou west born all was announced to me; wherefore blessed by the holy name of God. Jesus departed therefore that day from his mother to attend to his prophetic office. 1

The Holy Qur'an tells us the following: "And (I am) a verifier of that which is before me of the Torah, and I allow you part of that which was forbidden to you; and I have come to you with a sign from your Lord, so keep your duty to Allah and obey me. Surely Allah is my Lord and your Lord, so serve Him. This is the right path. 2

Sometime thereafter, Prophet Jesus delivered his first sermon, he ascended to the pulpit – the area where the scribes were accustomed speaking. The sermon he gave is as follows:

Then ascended Jesus to the place whence the scribes were wont to speak. And having beckoned with the hand for silence, he opened his mouth, saying: 'Blessed be the holy name of God, who of his goodness and mercy willed to create his creatures that they might glorify him. Blessed be the holy name of God, who created the splendor of all the saints and prophets before all things to send him for the salvation of the world, as he spoke by his servant David, saying: "Before Lucifer in the brightness of the saints I created thee." Blessed by the holy name of God, who created the angels that they might serve him. And blessed be God, who punished and reprobated Satan and his followers, who would not reverence him whom God willeth to be reverenced. Blessed be the holy name of God, who created man out of the clay of the earth, and set him over his works. Blessed be the holy name of God, who with mercy looked upon the tears of Adam and Eve, first parents of the human race. Blessed be the holy name of God who just punished Cain the fratricide, sent the deluge upon the earth. Burned up three wicked cities, scourged Egypt, overwhelmed Pharaoh in the Red Sea, scattered the enemies of his people, chastised the unbelievers and punished the impenitent. Blessed be the holy name of

God, who with mercy looked upon his creatures, and therefore sent them his holy prophets, that they might walk in truth and righteousness before him; who delivered his servants from every evil, and gave them this land, as he promised to our father Abraham and to his son forever. Then by his servant Moses he gave us his holy law, that Satan should not deceive us: and he exalted us above all other peoples.

'But, brethren, what do we to-day, that we be not punished for our sins?'

And then Jesus with greatest vehemence rebuked the people for that they had forgotten the word of God, and gave themselves only to vanity;

he rebuked the priests for their negligence in God's service and for their worldly greed; he rebuked the scribes because they preached vain doctrine, and forsook the law of God; he rebuked doctors because they made the law of God on none effect through their traditions. And in such wise did Jesus speak to the people, that all wept, form the least to the greatest, crying mercy, and beseeching Jesus that he would pray of them; save only their priests and leaders, who on that day conceived hatred against Jesus for having thus spoken against the priests, scribes, and doctors. And they meditated upon his death, but for fear of the people, who had received him as a prophet of God, they spoke no word.

Jesus raised his hands to the Lord God and prayed, and the people weeping said: 'So be it, O Lord, so be it.' The prayer being ended, Jesus descended from the temple; and that day he departed from Jerusalem, with many that followed him.

And the priests spoke evil of Jesus among themselves. 3
The Holy Qur'an states:
'He was naught but a servant on whom We bestowed favor and We made him an example for the Children of Israel.' 4

Jesus, according to the Gospels, had been raised as a Prophet of God with a three-fold objective;

1. To fulfill the Law

2. To "seek and save" the Lost Tribes of Israel

3. To proclaim the advent of the Paraclete

With regards to the Mosaic Law, Jesus had said:
'Think not that I am come to destroy the law, or the prophets: I am not come to destroy, but to fulfill. For verily I say unto you, Till heaven and earth pass, one jot or one title shall in no wise pass form the law, till all be fulfilled. Whosoever therefore shall break one of these least commandments, and shall teach men so, he shall be called the least in the kingdom of heaven: but whosoever shall do and teach them, the same shall be called great in the kingdom of heaven. For I say unto you, That except your righteousness shall exceed into the kingdom of heaven.' 5
When Jesus was questioned about the way of eternal, he said:
'Why callest thou me good? There is none good but one, that is, God: but if thou wilt enter into life, keep the commandments.' 6

It is clear, therefore that Jesus believed in and observed the law and asked his disciples to the same. According to him the Law and the Prophets were, and continued to be, the foundations of righteousness; and only by fulfilling their commandments was it possible to enter into the kingdom of heaven. The Gospels (Matthew, Mark, Luke, John, Barnabas, Thomas, Mary, etc..) are full of confirmations of the Law of Moses.

It should be noted here that Prophet Jesus chose twelve disciples;

The Gospel of St. Barnabas states:

'Jesus, seeing that great was the multitude of them (the people) that returned to their heart for, to walk in the law of God, went up into the mountain, and choose twelve, whom he called apostles, among whom I Judas, who was slain upon the cross. Their names are: Andrew and Peter his brother, fishermen; Barnabas, who wrote this, with Matthew the publican, who sat at the receipt of custom; John and James, sons of Zebedee; Thaddaeus and Judas; Bartholomew and Philip; James and Judas Iscariot the traitor. To these he always revealed the divine secrets; but the Iscariot Judas he made his dispenser of that which was given in alms, but he stole the tenth part of everything.' 7

The Israel of old believed themselves to be the chosen people of God; they considered Jehovah to be exclusively their God. Gradually, however there was a leaning towards universalism.

Jesus was not a universalist, even in this narrow sense; He had come with a Gospel to he house of Israel. In spite of the rejection of his Gospel by them he never preached to the Gentiles; for he said:

'It is not meet to take children's bread, and to cast it to dogs.'

And he declared also:

'For the son of man is come to save that which was lost.'

(see also Gospel of Luke 19:10)

Jesus was conscious of the limits and scopes of his mission. He knew that his message was meant only for the house of Jacob, the Israelites. He was aware of their glorious past, as the chosen people of God; and that Prophets had been raised amongst them for their guidance, which they had dis-believed, maltreated and persecuted, even killing some of them.

To his knowledge, the house of Jacob had, time and again, proved to be utterly unworthy of the trust thus reposed in them; and had rendered themselves unfit for future favors. He also knew that the Lord himself had said:

'For I am the Lord, I change not; therefore ye sons of Jacob are not consumed. Even from the days of your fathers ye are gone away from mine ordinances, and have not kept them. Return unto me, and I will return unto you, said the Lord of hosts. But he said, Wherein shall we return?\

Jesus not only cursed Israel, but he also cursed the important towns of Judea and Jerusalem, in particular, and thus made the significance of this curse absolutely clear. In this matter he was very precise and explicit.

He warned them:

'There I say unto you, The kingdom of God shall be taken from you, and given to a nation bringing forth the fruits thereof.' 11

Centuries earlier, God – Almighty had made a promise to Prophet Abraham and Hagar (Hajrah-daughter of the King of Egypt); and it was:

A NATION WILL BE RAISED FROM THEIR PROGENY AND GOD WILL BLESS THEM AND MAKE THEM GREAT.

Jesus belonged to the house of Jacob, was an Israelite and not an Ishmaelite. Therefore, this statement did not apply to him.

The Holy Prophet Muhammad was in direct line of descent from Ishmael. It is for this reason the Abraham has been styled as his father and also has been described as the progenitor of the Arabs. The Holy Qur'an records the following prayer of Abraham regarding the progeny of Ishmael:

'Our Lord, make us both submissive to Thee, and (raise) form our offspring, a nation submissive to Thee, and show us our ways of devotion and turn to us (mercifully); surely Thou art the Oft-returning (to mercy), the Merciful.' 12

Prophet Jesus also declared the following:

'And when Jesus, son of Mary, said: O children of Israel, surely I am the messenger of Allah to you, verifying that which is before me of the Torah and giving the good news of a Messenger who will come after me, his name being Ahmad. But when he came to them with clear arguments, they said: This is clear enchantment.' 13

The Gospel of St. Barnabas mentions in thirty-one places (approx.), the name of a messenger by the name of Muhammed, Islam's Holy Prophet and the Seal of the Prophets (Khatam-an-Nabiyyin).

However, there is a question that must be asked, what is the Gospel of St. Barnabas?

Barnabas was an Apostle of Jesus, selected by the Holy Spirit, an uncle of Mark the Evangelist, and a companion of Paul. He travelled throughout Palestine, from Damascus to Caesarea, and from Philipi to Mt. Sinai, preaching the gospel. His relics were discovered in a tomb in Cyprus in the fourth year of Emperor Zone (478 C.E.) and a copy of his Gospel, written in his own hand was found lying on his breast.

The Gospel of St. Barnabas was condemned by the Church by three successive Decrees:

1. Decree of the Western Church – 382 C.E…
2. Decree of Innocent – 465 C.E…
3. Decree of Gelasius – 496 C.E..

The Gelasius Decree mentions the EVANGELIUM BARNABAE in its index of the prohibited and heretical Gospels. The recovered Gospel gradually found its way to the library of Pope Sixtus V and it was found there in 1549 by a monk named Fra Marino.

The Gospel of St. Barnabas was accepted and read in the Churches up to Gelasian Decree. The Gospel contains a complete life of Jesus, his circumcision, the visit of the Magi, the Massacre of the Infants (his alleged –miraculous birth is also mentioned), the flight into and the return of the family form Egypt, and the discussion in the Temple. Its central portions deal with the journeys, miracles, discourses, parables and ethical and eschatological teachings of Jesus. Finally, it gives a description of the Paschal Supper and records the betrayal, the trial and the crucifixion.

The presence of the name Muhammad is really explained by the Aramaic equivalent, Mauhamana or the Greek word Paraclete, which John uses in his Gospel.

Jesus had therefore, foretold the future advent of the Paraclete, i.e., Mauhamana or Muhammed, the Messenger of God.

i.e., Mauhamana or Muhammad, the Messenger of God.

Paraclete, Comforter and Messiah is three and the same; these names belong to Prophet Muhammad (u.w.b.p.).

The Gospel of St. Barnabas, does not give a comprehensive insight into the sayings of Prophet Jesus; nevertheless the Holy Qur'an and this particular Gospel are only two of four places where 'some of the sayings' of Jesus can be found. The other sources where many, many, many sayings of Jesus can be found are: The Gospel of Thomas – The Hidden sayings of Jesus and The Unknown Life of Jesus Christ by Nicholas Notovitch.

Some of the sayings from the Gospel of Thomas are as follows:

1. Jesus said, "Look, the sower went out, took a handful of seeds, and scattered them. Some fell on the road, and the birds came and pecked them up. Others fell on rock, and they did

not take root in the soil and did not produce heads of grain. Others fell on thorns, and they choked the seeds and worms devoured them.

2. Jesus said, "A person was receiving guests. When he had prepared the dinner, he sent his servant to invite the guests. The servant went to the first and said to that one, "My master invites you." That person said, "Some merchants owe me money; they are coming to me tonight. I must go and give them instructions. Please excuse me from dinner." The servant went to another and said to that one, 'My master has invited you.' That person said to the servant, 'I have bought a house and I have been called away for a day. I shall have no time'. The servant went to another and said to that one, 'My master invites you'. That person said to to the servant, 'My friend is to be married and I am to arrange the banquet. I shall not be able to come. Please excuse me from dinner'. The servant went to another and said to that one, 'My master invites you'. That person said to the servant, 'I have bought an estate and I am going to collect the rent. I shall not be able to come. Please excuse'. The servant returned and said to his master, 'The people whom you invited to dinner have asked to be excused'.

The master said to his servant, 'Go out on the streets and bring back whomever you find to have dinner.

"Buyers and merchants will not enter the places of my father.'

3. Jesus said, "The kingdom is like a shepherd who had a hundred sheep one of them, the largest, went astray. He left the ninety-nine and sought the one until he found it. After he had gone to   this trouble, he said to the sheep, 'I love you more that the ninety-nine.'16

In chapter 95 of the same Gospel, Jesus vehemently stated the following:

Jesus said, "If you have money, do not lend it at interest. Rather, give it to someone from whom you will not get it back."

In the Unknown Life of Jesus by Nicholas Notovitch, the following sayings of many are mentioned:

1. "Enter into your temple, into your heart. Illumine it with good thoughts and the patience and immovable confidence

which you should have in your Father. And you sacred vessels, they are your hands and your eyes. See and do that which is agreeable to God, for in doing good to your neighbor you accomplish a rite which embellishes the temple wherein dwells he who gave life. For God has created you in his own likeness – innocent, with pure souls and hearts filled with goodness, destined not for the conception of evil schemes but made to be sanctuaries of love and justice.

Wherefore I say unto you, sully not your hearts, for the Supreme Being dwells therein eternally. If you wish to accomplish works marked with love or piety, do them with an open heart and let not your actions would not help to your salvation, and you would fall into that state of moral degradation where theft, lying and murder pass for generous deeds." 17

2. The elders then asked: "Who are you, and from what country does you come from? We have not heard you speak before, and we know not even your name." "I am an Israelite," replied Issa. "From the day of my birth I saw the walls of Jerusalem, and I heard the weeping of my brothers reduced to slavery and the lamentations of my sisters who were carried away by the pagans. And my soul was filled with sadness when I saw that my brethren had forgotten the true God. As a child, I left my father's house and went to dwell among other peoples. But having heard that my brethren were suffering still greater torments, I have come back to the country where my parents dwell to remind my brothers of the faith of their forefathers, which teaches us patience on earth to obtain perfect and sublime happiness in heaven.

3. And the learned elders put him this question: 'It is said that thou deniest the laws of Mossa and that thou teachest the people to forsake the temple of God?' And Issa replied: 'One cannot demolish that which has been given by our Heavenly Father, neither that which has been destroyed by sinners; but I have enjoined the purification of the heart from all blemish, for it is the true temple of God.

4. 'As to the laws of Mossa, I have endeavored to establish them in the hearts of men. And I say unto you that you do not understand their real meaning, for it is not vengeance but mercy that they teach: only the sense of these laws has been perverted." 18

It should be noted here, that these and many other sayings of Prophet Jesus are known as Parables; and at the same time, this great Prophet left a prayer for his followers; It is as follows:

"O Lord our God, hallowed be thy holy name, thy kingdom come in us, thy will be done always, and as it is done in heaven so be it done in earth; give us the bread for every day, and forgive us our sins, as we forgive them that sin against us, and suffer us not to fall into temptations, but deliver us from evil, for thou art alone our God, to whom pertaineth glory and honour for every." 19

It should be noted here that Prophet Jesus not only had twelve disciples but rater '82' (see Gospel of St. Barnabas ch. 100); of that figure we know of two-Nicodemus and Mary Magdalene: of which there are two Gospels written by them. However, it is Mary Magdalene that holds very special interest here.

The Prophet Jesus, it seems was in love or either he married the heir to the Throne of Solomon; the reason for this statement is the Gospel of Philip- ch. 49: Wisdom and Mary Magdala, and it reads;

'Wisdom, who is called barren, is the mother of the angels.

The companion of the savior is Mary Magdala. The savior loved her more than all the disciples, and he kissed her often on the mouth.

The other disciples... said to him, "Why do you love her more than all of us?"

The savior answered and said to them, "Why do I not love you like her? If a blind person and one who can see will see are both in darkness, they are the same. When the light comes, one who can see will see light, and the blind person will stay in darkness".'

Whatever really happened, we will never no the truth of Jesus and Mary Magdalene.

The history o religion tells us that whenever God sent his messengers to this world, the majority of the people opposed them and tried to put an end to their message. Jesus was therefore no exception. He therefore told the Children of Israel the following:

'Beware of the scribes, which desire to walk in synagogues, and the chief rooms in the market, and the highest seats in the synagogues, and the chief rooms at feasts; Which devour widows' houses, and for s hew make long prayers: the same shall receive greater damnation.' 20

Prophet Jesus was sent to re-unite, The Lost Tribes of Israel, with those already residing in Palestine. He was also sent to re-establish the Mosaic Law, give them the Gospel and give the good news of the coming of the Messiah; however non of this ever happened.

The next Chapter will explore what happened in year 33 A.D. (3rd year approximately on his ministry), the year of the 'attempted' crucifixion…..

LIST OF MIRACLES ATTRIBUTED TO PROPHET JESUS

The following list is a collection of miracles, attributed to Prophet Jesus and taken from various sources. The list may not be in chronological order and it may be incomplete.

Annunciation:
Luke 01:26-38// Holy Qur'an 03:44-51, 19:16-26.

Miraculous Baptism:
Matthew 03:13-17//Mark 01:09-11//Luke 03:21-22 //John 01:32-34

Prophet Jesus being protected by Angels in the desert:
Matthew 04:11//Mark 01:12-13

Nathanael's Miraculous Conversion:
John 01:45-51

Turned water into wine:
John 02:01-11

Exorcism in Capernaum:
Mark 01:21-28//Luke 04:31-37

Every disease healed:
Matthew 04:23-25//Mark 01:39

Large numbers of fish caught, and fisherman converted:
Luke 05:01-11

In the Prophet's name, demons exorcized and miracles performed:
Matthew 07:22//Mark 09:38-40, 16:17//Luke 09:49-50, 10:17// John
01:12-13, 02:23, 03:18, 14:13-14// Acts 03:06, 04:10&30, 16:18, 19:11-
20.

Cured a Leper:
Matthew 08:01-04// Mark 01:40-45//Luke 05:12-16

Conversion of a Samaritan woman:
John 04:28-29

A centurion's boy-servant cured:
Matthew 08:05-12//Luke 07:01-10

A royal official's son cured:
John 04:46-54.

Peter's mother-in-law's fever cured and evil spirits driven out:
Matthew 08:14-17//Mark 01:29-34//Luke 04:38-41.

A storm at sea calmed, the wind and waves rebuked:
Matthew 08:23-27//Mark 04:35-41\\Luke 08:22-25.
The Gerasene Demoniac, healed:
Matthew 08:28-34//Mark 05:01-20//Luke 08:26-39

Paralytic at Capernaum, cured:
Matthew 09:01-08//Mark 02:01-12//Luke 05:17-26

At a Pool of Bethesda, a parplytic cured:
John 05:01-18.

The son of a widow, raised at Nain:
Luke 07:11-17.

Jairus' daughter raised.........:
Matthew 09:18-26//Mark 05:25-43//Luke 08:40-56.

A woman who touched the fringes of his garment with a hemorrhage, healed:
Matthew 09:20-22//Mark 05:24-34//Luke 08:43-48

Two (2) blind men and a mute possessed with a spirit, healed:
Matthew 09:27-33.

Miracles at Chorazin, Bethsaida and Capernaum:
Matthew 11:20-24//Luke 10:13-15.

A withered man's hand, healed:
Matthew 12:09-13//Mark 03:01-06//Luke 06:06-11.

Hugh crowds, healed:
Matthew 12:15-21//Mark 03:07-12//Luke 06:17-19

A blind and dumb demoniac, healed:
Matthew 12:22-32//Mark 03:20-30//Luke 11:14-23 & 12:10

Fed 5000:
Matthew 14:13-21//Mark 06:30-44//Luke 09:10-17//John 06:01-14.

Walked on water:
Matthew 14:22-23//Mark 06:45-52//John 06:15-21

Those who touched the fringes of his garment were cured:
Matthew 14:34-36//Mark 06:53-56.

A Canaanite woman exorcised:
Matthew 15:21-28//Mark 07:24-30

A deaf man healed:
Mark 07:31-37.

Large numbers of crippled, blind and mute healed:
Matthew 15:29-31.

Fed 4000:

Matthew 15:32-39//Mark 08:01-10.

A man's sight restored at Bethsaida
Mark 08:22-26.

Transfiguration:
Matthew 17:01-13//Mark 09:02-13//Luke 09:28-36//2 Peter 01:17-18.

A possessed boy exorcised:
Matthew 17:14-21//Mark 09:14-29//Luke 09:37-43.

A woman healed on the Sabbath:
Luke 13:10-17

Even though Herod Antipas wanted him dead, he continued casting out demons:
Luke 13:31-32.

A man with dropsy, healed:
Luke 14:01-06.

Ten lepers healed:
Luke 17:11-19

Large crowds healed in Judea:
Matthew 19:01-02.

Two blind men, healed:
Matthew 20:29-34.

Bartimaeus, the blind beggar, healed:
Mark 10:46-52//Luke 18:35-43.

Gave a blind man sight:
John 09.

At Herod's Temple, the blind and lame healed:
Matthew 21:14.

A fig tree, cursed:
Matthew 21:18-22//Mark 11:12-14 & 20-25.

The last supper:
Matthew 26:26-30//Mark 14:22-26//Luke 22:14-20//John 06:48-66\\1 Corinthians 11:23-26

The Messiah, Jesus Christ is betrayed by Judas Iscariot:
John 13:26-30

The High Priest's servant's ear, reattached and healed
Luke 22:49-51.

Solar Eclipse:
Matthew 27:45\\Mark 15:30\\Luke 23:44-45//\Gospels of Peter & Nicodemus.

An empty tomb:
Matthew 27:62-28:15//Mark 16:01-08//Luke 24:01-12//John 20:10-10\\Gospel of Peter 08:01-13:03.

Appearances after the Crucifixion:
Matthew 28:09-10 & 16-20//Mark 16:09-18//Luke 24:13-49//John 20:11-23\\Acts 01:01-08 & 02:24//Romans 10:09//1 Corinthians 09:01-15.

LIST OF PARABLES AS TOLD BY PROPHET JESUS

The following list is a collection of Parables, as told by Prophet Jesus and is taken from various sources. The list may not be in chronological order and it may be incomplete.

Salt and Light
Matthew 05:13-16//Mark 09:50//Luke 14:34-35//Gospel of St. Thomas 32-33.

The Candlestick:
Mark 04:21//Luke 08:16 & 11:33.

The Defendant:
Matthew 05:25-26//Luke 12:58-59//Gospel of St. Thomas 91.

The Birds of Heaven:
Matthew 06:26//Luke 12:24//Gospel of St. Thomas 36.

Lilies of the Field:
Matthew 06:28-30//Luke 12:27-28.

The Mote and the Beam:
Matthew 07:01-05.

The Test of a Good Person:
Matthew 07:15-20//Luke 06:43-45//Gospel of St. Thomas 45.

The Wise and the Foolish Builders:
Matthew 07:24-27//Luke 06:47-49.

The Patch and the Wineskin:
Matthew 09:16-17//Mark 02:21-22//Luke 05:36-39//Gospel of St. Thomas 47.

The Strong Man Bound:
Matthew 12:29//Mark 03:27//Luke 11:21-22//Gospel of St. Thomas 35.

Jesus' True Relatives:
Matthew 12:46-50//Mark 03:31-35//Luke 08:19-21//Gospel of St. Thomas 99.

The Sower:
Matthew 13:03-23//Mark 04:01-20//Luke 08:05-15//Gospel of St. Thomas 09.

The Tares:
Matthew 13:24-30//Gospel of St. Thomas 57

The Mustard Seed:

Matthew 13:31-32//Mark 04:30-32//Luke 13:18-19//Gospel of St. Thomas 20.

The Leaven:
Matthew 13:33//Luke 13:20-21//Gospel of St. Thomas 96.

The Hidden Treasures:
Matthew 13:44//Gospel of St. Thomas 109.

Story of the Pearl:
Matthew 13:45-46//Gospel of St. Thomas 76.

The Net:
Matthew 13:47-50//Gospel of St. Thomas 08.

The Teacher of the Law:
Matthew 13:52.

The Little Children;
Matthew 18:01-10//Mark 09:33-37 & 42-50//Luke 09:46-50//Gospel of St. Thomas 22.

The Lost Sheep:
Matthew 18:12-14//Luke 15:03-07//Gospel of St. Thomas 107.

Unmerciful Servant:
Matthew 18:23-35.

Laborers in the Vineyard:
Matthew 20:01:15.

The Two Sons:
Matthew 21:28-31.

The Wicked Husbandman:
Matthew 21:33-43//Mark 12:01-11//Luke 20:09-18//Gospel of St. Thomas 65-66.

The Marriage of the King's Son:
Matthew 22:01-14/Luke 14:15-24//Gospel of St. Thomas 64.

Give unto Caesar:
Matthew 22:15-22//Mark 12:13-17//Luke 20:20-26//Gospel of St. Thomas 100.

The Fig Tree:
Matthew 24:32//Mark 13:28//Luke 21:29-30.

The Faithful Servants:
Matthew 24:42//Mark 13:33-37//Luke 12:35-40//Gospel of St. Thomas 21 & 103.

The Ten Virgins:
Matthew 25:01-12.

The Talents:
Matthew 25:01-12.

The Sheep and the Goats:
Matthew 25:31-46.
Growing seed secretly:
Mark 04:26-29//Gospel of St. Thomas 21.

The Two Debtors:
Luke 07:41-47.

The Good Samaritan:
Luke 10:30-37.

The Night Friend:
Luke 11:05-08.

The Rich Fool:
Luke 12:16-21//Gospel of St. Thomas 63.

The Barren Fig Tree:
Luke 13:06-09.

Monkey Lost:
Luke 15:08-09.

The Prodigal Son:
Luke 15:11-32.

The Unjust Steward:
Luke 16:01-08.

Lazarus and the Rich Man:
Luke 16:19-31.

Master and Servant:
Luke 17:07-10.

The Importunate Widow:
Luke 18:01-08.

Pharisee and the Publican:
Luke 18:09-14.

Paraclete/Holy Spirit:
Matthew 03:10-12//Mark 01:08//Luke 03:16-17//John 14:16, 26;15:26
& 16:07//Acts 01:05, 08;02:04,38;11:16//Holy Qur'an 61:06.

CHAPTER 05

An Event Unravelled

The year is 33 AD. Many Biblical Scholars have declared that this particular year is, the Year of the Passion of Christ.

It is also, the year when Pontius Pilate, the fifth (5th.) governor of the Roman province of Judaea, makes his biblical appearance. Pilate's rule began in 26 C.E. and ended in 37 C.E.

Pontius Pilate was married to a woman named Procla, who was originally from Gaul. Historically and Coincidentally, Pilate is mentioned by the Jewish writer Flavius Josephus, who composed his two great works entitled;

1. The Antiquities of the Jews   2.   The Jewish War.

Pilate wasn't 100% evil, as many would want him to be. He was merely a 'bad' cherry or grape, that one should avoid. One thing is certain, he seems to had an intuition, about the coming of the King of the Jews', or the coming of the Messiah; both titles being both one and the same.

Our look at Prophet Jesus, takes us to the Passover festival, which was drawing near, and large numbers of people began preparations to visit Jerusalem to commemorate the delivery of the Jews from bondage, in Egypt several hundreds of years earlier. This is an important Jewish festival, in which. Orthodox Jews abstain from eating leavened bread during this special festival. Instead they use unleavened bread in the form of matzoth. By eating matzoth, they recall the unleavened bread eaten by the Israelites during their flight, because they didn't have time to prepare raised bread. During Passover, meals are also prepared and served using sets of utensils and dishes reserved strictly for this festival.

It is said that Prophet Jesus went to Jerusalem on this occasion. He rode a donkey that was provided by his disciples, and entered Jerusalem. The crowd greeted him, listened to him and they were very impressed by what He had to say. The Bible tells us the following;

"And when he had come into Jerusalem, all the city was moved, saying, Who is this? And the multitude said, This is Jesus the Prophet of Nazareth of Galilee."1

The chief priests and the teachers of the Law heard the reporters of his growing influence and became very worried. It is possible that they had persuaded the authorities to arrest Jesus Christ, whilst he was in Jerusalem.

"Then assembled together the chief priests, and the scribes, and the elders of the people, unto the place of the High Priest, who was called Caiaphas, and consulted that they might take Jesus by subtility, and kill him. But they said, "Not on the feast day, lest there be an uproar among the people."2

The Prophet Jesus was aware of their plans. He took necessary precautions but remained in Jerusalem and continued delivering the message of Allah to the people.

In the evening, when the hour come, he sat down with the twelve (12) disciples or apostles. Then he said to them:

"With anticipation, I have desired to eat this Passover with you before I supper. I say to you, I will not eat any more thereof until it be fulfilled in the Kingdom of God."3

While they were sitting, Jesus continued:

"Truly, I say to you that one of you who eats with me shall betray me. They began to be sorrowful and to inquire amongst themselves, as to who should do this thing. One by one, they asked, 'Lord, is it I?'

He answered, It is one of the Twelve that dips his hand with me in the dish. Truly, the son of man goes as it was determined, but woe to that man by whom he is betrayed! It were good for that man if he had not been born!"4

Then Judas Iscrariot, who betrayed him, asked, Master is it I?

Jesus replied, You have said it.

As they were eating, Jesus took bread, and blessed it, broke it and gave it to the disciples, and said, Take, eat; this is my body which is given for you; this do in remembrance of me. Then he took the cup and gave thanks, and he gave it to them, saying; Take this, and divide it, and drink all of you of this.

They all drank it. Then he said, This is my blood of the New Covenant which is shed for many for the Remission of Sins. I say to you, I will not drink henceforth of this fruit of the vine until that day when I drink it anew with you in my Father's Kingdom.

At this juncture, the following should be mentioned and noted:

Prophet Jesus was accustomed to spending many a night atop of Mount of Olives, with many of his disciples. However many hours before he was to be betrayed, Prophet Jesus was giving his disciples, an insight into understanding the Gospel. He said unto them:

" All of you shall be offended of me this night, for it is written, 'I will smite the shepherd, And the sheep of the flock shall be scattered.'

However, after I am risen again, I will go before you into Galilee.

Peter said to him, Though all men shall be offended because of you, yet I will never be offended. Then Jesus said, Simon, Simon, behold, Satan has desired to have that he may sift you as wheat. However, I have prayed for you that your faith does not fail, and, when you are converted, strengthen your brothers.

Simon replied, Lord I am ready to go with you both to prison and to death. Jesus responded, I tell you, Peter, that this day, even in this night, before the cock crows twice, you shall deny that you know me trice.

Peter spoke more forcefully, Though I should die with you, yet I will not deny you in any way. Likewise, all the disciples said the same.

Jesus continued, When I sent you without purse, and bag, and shoes, did you lack anything? They answered, Nothing.

Then he said to them, But now, he that has a purse, let him take it, and likewise, his bag; he that has no sword, let him sell his garment and buy one.

I say to you, this that is written must yet be accomplished in me, for the things concerning me have a purpose: 'He was reckoned among the transgressors.'

Then they said, Lord, behold, here are two swords."

Before going to the gardens of Gethsemane, the following took place:

Pilate had a Roman guard sent to seek out Jesus. After seeking out Jesus, the guard then escorted Jesus to Pontius Pilate, at which the Governor said:

"Young man, I have a word to say that may be well for you. I have observed your works and words for three years and more; And I have often stood in your defense when your own countrymen would gladly of stoned you as a criminal. But now the priests, the scribes and Pharisees have stirred the common people to a stage of frenzied wantonness and cruelty, and they intend to take your life. Because, they say, that you have sworn to tear their temple down; to change the laws that Moses gave; to exile Pharisee and priest and seat yourself upon a throne. And they aver that you are fully in league with Rome.

The streets of all Jerusalem are filled this moment with a horde of madmen all intent to shed your blood. There is no safety for you but in flight; wait not until the morning sun. You know the way to reach the border of this cursed land. I have a little and of guards, well horsed and armed, and they will take you out beyond the reach of harm. You must not tarry here, young man, you must arise and go.

And Jesus said,

A noble prince has Caesar in his Pontius Pilate, and from the point of carnal man your words are seasoned with the wise man's salt; but from the point of Christ words are foolishness. The coward flees when danger comes; but he who comes to seek and save the lost must give his life in willing sacrifice for those he comes to seek and save. Before the pasch has been consumed, lo, all nation will be cursed b shedding blood of innocent; and even now the murderers are at the door.

And Pilate said,

It shall not be; the sword of Rome will be unsheathed to save your life.

And Jesus said,

Nay, Pilate, nay; there are no armies large enough in all the world to save my life."

And is was here that Jesus bade farewell to Pilate and disappeared into the darkness of the night.5

After leaving the company of Pontius Pilate, Jesus made his way to the gardens of Gethsemane, where he took with him Peter, James and John; and where the following took place:

When they arrived at Gethsemane, 'And he was withdrawn from the about a stone's cast, and he kneeled down, and prayed, saying, Father, if thou be willing remove this cup from me: nevertheless not my will, but thine, be done.

And there appeared an angel unto him from heaven, strengthening him.

And being in an agony he prayed more earnestly: and his sweat was as it were great drops of blood falling down to the ground.

And when he rose up from prayer, and was com to his disciples, he found them sleeping for sorrow, and said unto them, Why sleep, you'll? Rise and pray, lest you'll enter into temptation.'6

Also........

He went away again the second time, and prayed, saying; O my Father, if this cup may not pass away from me, except I drink it, thy will be done.

And he came and found them asleep again: for their eyes were heavy.

And he left them, and went away again and prayed the third time, saying the same words. Then cometh he to his disciples, and said unto them, Sleep on now, and take your rest: behold, the hour is at hand, and the Son of man is betrayed into the hands of sinners.7

Is should also be mentioned at this juncture, that Judas Iscrariot, an apostle of Jesus betrayed him, knew the place: for Jesus ofttimes resorted together with his disciples. Judas then, having received a band of men and officers from the chief priests and Pharisees, came together with lanterns and torches and weapons.'8

NEXT....

Then the band and the captain and officers of the Jews took Jesus, and bound him, and led him away to Annas first; for he was father-in-law to Caiaphas, which was the high priest that year.

Annas then questioned him in his own way (see John 18 – Verses 13-23).

'Now Annas had sent him bound unto Caiaphas the high priest.9

At this juncture, it should be mentioned, that when Jesus is brought before Caiaphas, the High Priest, there was no trial at this point in time. What takes place here, is actually an Arraignment of the accused. The next day being his trial!

The Chief Priests and all the Council sought at this arraignment, for witnesses, who would give false testimony against Prophet Jesus. The false testimonies would eventually lead to Jesus, being put to death.

At least, two false witnesses came and testified against him saying:

"We heard this fellow say, I will destroy this Temple of God that is made with hands and within three days, I will build another made without hands."

Later, the High Priest asked him:

"I adjure you by the Living God that you tell us weather you are the Messiah, the Son of the Blessed?

Jesus answered: you say it. Hereafter, you shall see the Son of Man sitting on the Right Hand of the Power of God and coming in the Clouds of Heaven.

Then the High Priest ripped his clothes and said, Why need we any further witnesses? You have heard the blasphemy out of his own mouth! What do you think?

They answered in condemnation, He is guilty of death!

Some of the men that held Jesus began to spit on him, and to cover his face, and to buffet him: the servants blindfolded him, and struck him on the face with the palms of their hands and they said to him, Prophesy to us, Messiah, who is it that smote you!"

Enter Peter, who was below in the palace, there came one of the maids of the High Priest. When she saw Peter warming himself, she looked carefully at him and said, 'This fellow was also with Jesus of Nazareth.'

He denied it in front of all of them, saying, 'Woman, I do not know him, nor do I understand what you say.'

Then he went into the porch, and the cock crew. Another maid saw him and began to say to them that stood by, 'This is one of them: he was also with him!' Again, he denied it with an oath, "I am not!'

About an hour after, they that stood by said again to Peter, 'Surely, you are one of them, for you are a Galilean, and your speech betrays it.'

Then he began to curse and to swear, saying, 'Man, I do not know what you are talking about! And I do not know this man!

Immediately, the cock crew the second time, and the Lord turned and looked at Peter. He called to mind the words that Jesus had said to him, 'Before the cock crow twice, you shall deny me trice.'

When he thought about it, he went out and wept bitterly.

At this juncture, the following must be mentioned, from The Gospel of Judas:

"Judas said to Jesus, What is the long duration of time that the human being will live? Jesus said, Why are you wondering about this, that Adam, with his generation, has lived his span of life in the place were he has received his kingdom, with his ruler?

Judas said to Jesus, Does the human spirit die?

58

Jesus said, This is why God ordered Michael to give the spirits of people to them as a loan, so that they might offer service, but the Great One ordered

Gabriel to grant spirits to the great generation with no ruler over it – that is, the spirit and the soul. Therefore, the rest of the souls (-one line missing-)."

I mentioned the above because, I want my readers to note the following, that the disciple named Judas Iscariot, even though Christianity portrays him as the traitor, bastard and villain, he was actually a hero.

A hero that betrayed the Prophet Jesus at the eleventh hour, however, during his tenureship, as a disciple, he obeyed everything the Master said. Technical questions and statements about Religion, Judas understood what was being discussed.

That is why, when Judas betrayed the Prophet, and actually hearing and seeing his master being condemned, he opted to repent, ans as such, brought back the thirty pieces of silver to the Chief Priests and Elders saying:

"I have sinned in that I have betrayed the Blood of the Innocent.

They responded, What is that to us? You see to it!

So he cast down the pieces of silver in the Temple and departed, and he went and hanged himself. Then the Chief Priests took the silver pieces and said. It is not lawful to put them into the treasury because it is the price of blood. They took counsel and bought with them the Potter's Field in which to bury strangers. Therefore, that field was called the field of blood unto this day.

Then was fulfilled that which was spoken by Prophet Jeremiah, viz:

"They took the thirty pieces of silver,

The Price of him that was valued,

Whom they of the children of Israel did value,

And gave them for the Potter's field,

As the Lord appointed me."10

The Aquarian Gospel of Jesus the Christ, tells us in Chapter 167, the following, in verses 01-05:

'Into the place of the Roman Governor the Jews would enter not lest they become defiled and be unworthy to attend the feast; but they led Jesus to the place court, and Pilate met them there. And Pilate said, Why this commotion in the early day? What is your prayer?

The Jews replied, We bring before you one, an evil and seditious man.

He has been tried before the highest council of the Jews and has been proven traitor to our laws, our state and to the government of Rome.

We pray that you will sentence him to death upon the cross.'

The King James, New Testament Bible tells us the following:

When Pilate heard the charges against Jesus he said to them;

Take ye him, and judge him according to your law. The Jews therefore said unto him, It is not lawful for us to put any man to death."11

The accusations brought on by the Jews, onto Prophet Jesus continued;

We found this fellow perverting the nation, and forbidding to give tribute to Caesar, saying that he himself is Christ is King.12

Pontius Pilate asked the Prophet Jesus, Are you the King of Jews?

And Jesus responded by saying;

"My Kingdom is not of this world: if my Kingdom were of this world, then would my servants fight, there I should not be delivered to the Jews: but now is my Kingdom not from hence."13

Then Pilate said to the chief priests and the crowds, 'I find no reason to condemn this men.'

But they insisted even more strongly, 'With his teaching he is starting a riot among the people all through Judaea. He began in Galilee and now has come here.

When Pilate heard of Galilee, he asked whether the man were a Galilaean. And as soon as he knew that he belonged unto Herod's jurisdiction, he sent him to Herod, who himself also was at Jerusalem at that time.

And when Herod saw Jesus, he was exceeding glad: for he was desirous to see him of a long season, because he had heard many things of him; and he hoped to have seen some miracle done by him.

Then he questioned with him in many words; but he answered him nothing.

And the chief priests and scribes stood and vehemently accused him.

And Herod with his men of war set him at nought, and mocked him, and arrayed him in gorgeous robe, and sent him again to Pilate."14

Pontius Pilate was convinced beyond any doubt that Jesus was innocent, therefore he tried to set him free but the Jews protested violently.

"And Pilate, when he had called together the chief priests and rulers and the people. Said unto them, 'Ye have brought this man unto me, as one that perverth the people: and behold, I having examined him before you, have found no fault in this man touching those things whereof ye accused him:'

No, nor yet Herod: for I sent you to him; and, lo, nothing worthy of death is done unto him. I will therefore chastise him, and release him."15

The Jews insisted that he was a traitor and therefore should be hanged, they also placed alot of pressure on Pilate, so that he could not set Jesus free though he was still anxious to save his life. During the trial, Pilate's wife met him in an inner room, silence in thinking, she told him the following:

"I pray you, Pilate, hearken unto me: Beware of what you do this hour. Tough not this man from Galilee; he is a holy man.

If you should scourge this man, you scourge the sun of God. Last night I saw it all in vision far too vivid to be set aside as idle dream.

I saw this man walk on the waters of the sea; I heard him speak and calm an angry storm; I saw him flying with the wings of light;

I saw Jerusalem in blood; I saw the statues of Ceasars fall; I saw a veil before the sun, and day was dark as night.

The earth on which I stood was shaken like a reed before the wind. I tell you, Pilate, if you bathe your hands in this man's blood then you may dread the frowns of great Tiberius, an curses of the senators of Rome."16

Pilate's wife left and Pilate, broke down and wept.

At this point, Pilate made yet another attempt to persuade the Jews to have the Messiah, Jesus Christ – son of Mary and Joseph, released.

He gave the enraged crowd an option, either to save the life of Jesus or that of a 'notorious' criminal called Barabbas (it is alleged, that Barabbas was a Zealot). The Bible tells us thus;

"Now at that feast the governor was accustomed to release unto the people a prisoner, whom they would. And they had, then a notable prisoner, called Barabbas. Therefore when they were gathered together, Pilate said unto them,

'Whom will ye that I release unto you? Barabbas, or Jesus which is called Christ?' "17

They answered, BARABBAS, because the chief priests and the elders had persuaded the crowds to ask Pilate to set Barabbas free and have Jesus put to death.

"And the governor said, Why, what evil hath he done? But they cried out the more, saying, Let him be crucified."18

They even threatened to writhe to Caesar, that Pilate had set free a person who claimed to be a King, which meant that Pilate himself was also a rebel against the Emperor.

"When Pilate saw that he could prevail nothing, but that rather a tumult was made, he took water, and washed his hands before the multitude, saying, I am innocent of the blood of this just person: see ye to it.

Then answered all the people, and said, His blood be on us, and on our children."19

"And Pilate gave sentence that it should be as they required. And he released unto them him that for sedition and murder was cast into prison, whom they had desired; but he delivered Jesus to their will."20

This act on the part of Pilate, amounts to confession that Jesus was indeed innocent and under duress. It is quite clear from the Biblical account that the Jewish community had colluded against Jesus and were determined to the Jewish clergy would have resulted in a riot.

Friday afternoon was fixed (and not Wednesday), as the day of the Crucifixion.

Jesus prayed:

"Father, my Father! All things are possible for you. Take this cup of suffering away from me."

He prayed fervently because the truth of his claim was at stake. Jesus know that if the Jews succeeded in their attempt to kill him by crucifixion, they would proclaim him to be an imposter, whose falsehood had finally been proven on the authority of divine scripture, which says;

"His body shall not remain all night upon the tree, but thou shall in any wise bury him that day; (for he that is hanged is accursed of God;) that thy land be not defiled, which the Lord thy God giveth thee for an inheritance."21

the prayers of Jesus was accepted and God assured him that he would be saved from the accursed death on the cross. According to the Holy Qur'an, God (Allah) told him;

"When Allah said: O Jesus, I will cause thee to die and exalt thee in My presence and clear thee of those who disbelieve to the day of Resurrection. Then to Me is your return, so I shall decide between you concerning that wherein you differ."22

The Bible too seemed to have given a similar message.

When the Jews demanded a sign from Jesus, he replied;

"An evil and adulterous generation seeketh after a sign: and there shall no sign be given to it, but the sign of the prophet Jonas: For as Jonas was three nights in the whale's belly; so shall the Son of man be three days and three nights in the heart of the earth."23

The Holy Qur'an also gives us the following:

"And Jonas was surely of those sent. When he fled to the laden ship, So he shared with others but was of those cast away.

So the fish took him into its mouth while he was blamable. But had he not been of those who glorify (Us), He would have tarried in its belly till the day when they are raised. Then We cast him. And We sent him to a hundred thousand or more."24

On Friday morning, the said day of the crucifixion, there was a huge commotion in the city. Most of the enemies of Jesus were looking forward to It should be noted here, the following took place;

"Then Pilate commend Jesus to be brought before him, and spoke to him in the following words:

'Thy own nation has charged thee as making thyself a king; wherefore I, Pilate sentence thee to be wipped according to the laws of former governors; and that thou be first bound, then hanged upon a cross in that place where there is now a prisoner; and also two criminals with thee, whose names are Dimas and Gestas.'"25

Also, According to the Bible, a crown of thorny branches was put on his head and he was beaten and spat at. Jesus was taken to Golgotha, the place of execution (about 600m away). A great crowd followed him through the streets, jeering at him and hurling insults at him.

The Gospel, according to John, tells us that he carried his own cross. According to the Jewish custom, which was fully endorsed by the Roman Law, nobody was permitted to remain on the cross on the Sabbath. The Sabbath begins at sunset on Friday and remains up to sunset on Saturday.

In those days, the hands and feet of the condemned persons were nailed to wooden cross, and no food was served to them, so they were used to dying of hunger and thirst. Death was the result of a slow process which sometimes took three or four days. It was also a practice that the soldiers would break the leg bones of the victims to ensure their death.

There is an historical document, which was compiled into a book, that book is entitled, 'The Crucifixion by an Eyewitness.'

This book, was actually a Latin manuscript, which was found in the form of a letter written in Alexandria – Egypt, in the 19th century. The letter in question, was written by an elder of the Essene Brotherhood in Jerusalem to his Essene brethen in Alexandria, in reply to their letter inquiring the truth about Jesus, whom they had heard rumors. The letter was written seven years after the events of the cross. The following is mentioned in the aforementioned Book: "Jesus was pierced through with thick iron nails, but not his feet. This seems credible as otherwise, Jesus would not have been able to journey on foot onto the road of Emmaus. On Sunday evening so soon after being nailed to the cross."

Let's return to the events of that faithful Friday afternoon........

The cross was put up on the hill of Golgotha, outside the city wall of Jerusalem. A crowd had gathered there to witness the unfolding events.

Mary, his mother, Mary – the Magdalene of Magdala and one or two of his disciples and well wishers of Jesus were also present.

"And they that passed by reviled him, wagging their heads."26

"Likewise also the chief priests mocking him, with the scribes and elders, said,

He saved others; himself he cannot save. If he be the King of Israel, let him now come down from the cross, and we will believe him."27

"And about the ninth hour Jesus cried with a loud voice, saying, 'Eli Eli lama aa-bach-tha-ni? 'My God, My God, why has thou forsaken me?.28

According to the Nazarean Essences, in their Book, 'The Crucifixion by an Eyewitness:

"Darkness descended over the earth, an the people returned to Jerusalem, the leaders of our holy order remained on in Golgotha, our order having nearby a colony for worship and for partaking of feast of love."

Then he (Jesus) said, I thirst: "A Roman soldier dipped a sponge in vinegar and myrrh, and placed it to his lips."29

'The Crucifixion by an Eyewitness, also states: "As he (the Centurion) recommended his mother (Mary), to the care of John – The Evangelist, it was growing darker, although the full moon should have been shinning in the heavens.

From the Dead Sea, was observed a thick rise of a reddish fog. The mountain ridges in the vicinity of Jerusalem shook violently, and the head of Jesus sand down upon his breast.

When he uttered his last groan of pain and passed away, a hissing sound was heard in the air; and they the Jews that remained where seized by a great fear for they believed that the evil spirits who dwell between heaven and earth were proceeding to punish the people. It was that stranger and unusual sound were proceedes an Earthquake."

At this juncture, another interesting source, mentions the following:

"The centurion went to the governor, and related to him all that had passed; And calling the Jews heard, they answered to the governor, The eclipse of the sun happened according to its usual custom.:30

As the Sabbath was approaching, the soldiers broke the legs of the two bandits, who were still alive at that time. They died when their legs were broken, but when they came to Jesus, they thought that he had already died."Then Longinus,a certain soldier,taking a spear,pierced his side,and presently there came fort blood and water." 31' The rushing of blood and water from his body was a proof that Jesus was alive at that moment and not dead, as Medical Science tells us that blood and water cannot gush forth fro ma dead body.' If he was dead and his hearth had stopped beating, such active bleeding as causing the blood to gush out would be impossible.

Surprisingly the legs of Jesus were not broken.

'The Crucifixion by an Eyewitness, states further, the following:

"There was a certain Joseph, from Arimathea. He was rich, and being a member of the council, he was much esteemed by the people. He was a prudent man, and whilst he did not appear to belong to any party, he was secretly a member of our sacred Order and lived in accordance with our laws. His friend Nicodemus was a most learned man, and belonged to the highest degree of our order.

He knew the secrets of the 'Terapeuts,' and was often together with us.

Now it so happened that after the earthquake, and many of the people had gone away, Joseph and Nicodemus arrived at the cross. They were informed of the death of the crucified, in the garden of our Brethren, not far from Calvary.

Although they loudly lamented his fete, it nevertheless appeared strange to them that Jesus, having hung less that seven hours, should already be dead. They could not believe it, and hastily went up to the place. There they found John alone, he determined to see what became of the beloved body.

Joseph and Nicodemus examined the body of Jesus, and Nicodemus, greatly moved, drew Joseph aside and said to him: 'As sure my knowledge of life and nature, so sure it is possible to save him.'

But Joseph did not understand him, and he admonished us that we should not tell John of what we had heard. Indeed, it was a secret to save our Brother from death. Nicodemus shouted: 'We must immediately have his body with its bones unbroken, because he may still saved ', then, realizing his want of caution, he continued in a whisper,'saved from being infamously buried.'

He persuaded Joseph to disregard his won interest, that he might save their Friend by going immediately to Pilate, and prevailing upon him to permit them to take Jesus' body from the cross that very night and put it in the sepulcher, hewn in the rock close by, and which belonged to Joseph."

The Bible also mentions the coming and going of the disciples to the tomb but everything was done with great caution and in secrecy.

The Gospel of Luke – Chapter 23 Verses 55-56 mentions the following:

"And the women also, which came with him from Galilee, followed after, and beheld the sepulcher, and how his body was laid. And they returned, and prepared spices and ointments; and rested the sabbath day according to the commandment."

The Ointment which was prepared in advance, was applied to the wounds of Prophet Jesus. All the ingredients of this ointment, has properties of healing wounds and subduing pain. This ointment was known as the 'MARHAM-I-ISH' or the Ointment of Jesus.

Hadhrat Mirza Ghulam Ahmad of Qadian, India and Holy Founder of the Ahmaddiyyat Sect of Islam, wrote a book, 'Jesus in India' in 1899 in which he declared that Jesus did not ascend to heaven as was believed by the Christians as well as the major section of the Muslim community. He was saved from the accursed death on the cross, migrated to the countries where the lost tribes of Israel had settled. How did the Messiah, defeat death, the first time?

Well, if my dear readers would read on, the truth would be revealed.

In, Hadhrat Mirza's book, Chapter 03: 'On the evidence derived from books of Medicine,' the following should be noted: "A   piece   of evidence of great value with regard to the escape of Jesus from the Cross, which no one can help admitting, is a medical preparation known as Marham-i-Isa or the 'Ointment of Jesus' recorded in hundreds of medical books. Some of these books were complied by Christians, some of Magians or Jews, some by Muslims. Most ot them are very old. Investigations show that in the beginning, the preparation came to be known as an oral tradition among hundreds of thousands of people. Then they recorded it.

At first, in the very time of Jesus, a little after the event of the Cross, a pharmaceutical work was compiled in Latin, in which there was a mention of this preparation along with the statement that the preparation had been prepared along with the statement that the preparation had been prepared for the wounds of Jesus.

Five (5) rare books that mention the Marham-i-Isa are:

1. Ijala-i-Nafiah by Muhamed Sharif Dehlavi, page 410.

2. Tibb-i-Akbar by Muhammed Akbar Arzani, page 242.

3. Hadi Kabir by Ibn-i-Zakariya, Skin Diseases.

4. Shifa-il-Asqam: Volume II, page 230.

5. Qanun by Shaikh-ul-Rais Bu Ali Sina: Volume III, page 133.

The Crucifixion by an Eyewitness, gives us the following:

"These spices and salves had great healing powers, and were used by our Essene Brethen who knew the rules of medical science for the restoration to consciousness of those in a state of deathlike fainting.

And even as Joseph Nicodemus were bending over his face and their tears fall upon him, they blew into him their own breath, and warmed his temples.

Still Joseph was doubtful of his recovery to life, but Nicodemus encouraged him to increase their efforts. Nicodemus spread balsam in both the nail pierced hands, but he believed that it was not best to close up the wound in Jesus' side, because he considered the flow of blood and water therefrom helpful to respiration and beneficial in the renewing of life.

The body was then laid in the sepulcher made in the rocks which belonged to Joseph. They then smoked the grotto with aloe and other strengthening herbs, and while the body lay upon the bed of moss, still stiff and inanimate, they placed a large stone in front of the entrance, that the vapours might better fill the grotto."

The Jews themselves were not sure of the death of Jesus. They remembered the prophecy that Jesus had made that he would show that the miracle of Jonah and would come out of the heart of the earth alive.

Therefore the chief priests and the Pharisees went again to Pilate and said to him, the following:

"Sir, we remember that that deceiver said, while he was yet alive, After three days I will rise again. Command therefore that the sepulcher be made sure until the third day, lest his disciples come by night, and steal him away, and say unto the people, He is risen from the dead: so the last error shall be worse than the first. Pilate said unto them, Ye have a watch: go your way, make it sure as you can. So they went, and made the sepulcher sure, sealing the stone, and setting a watch."32

The Crucifixion by an Eyewitness, states the following:

"One of our brethen went to the grave, in obedience to the the order of the Brotherhood, dressed in the white robe of the fourth degree. He went by way of a secret path which ran through the mountain to the grave, and which was known only to the order..

When the timid servants of the high priest saw the white robed Brother on the mountain slowly approaching, and partially obscured by the morning mist, they were seized with a great fear and they thought that an angel was descending from the mountain.

When this brother arrived at the grave which he was to guard, he rested on the stone which he had pulled from the entrance according to his orders; whereupon the soldiers fled and spread the report than angel had driven them away.

Thirty hours had now passed since the assumed death of Jesus. And when the Brother, having heard a slight noise within the grotto, went in to observe what had happened, he smelled a strange odour in the air, such as often occurs when the earth is about to vomit forth fire.

And the youth observed with inexpressible joy that the lips of the body moved, and that it breathed. He at once hastened to Jesus to assist him, and heard slight sound rising from his breast. The face assumed a living appearance, and the eyes opened and in astonishment gazed at the novice of our Order.

This occurred just as I was leaving with the brethren of the first degree, from the council, with Joseph, who had come to consult how to bring help.

Nicodemus, who was an experienced physician, said, on the way, that the peculiar condition of the atmosphere caused by the revolution of the elements was beneficial to Jesus, and that he never had believed that Jesus was really dead. And he further said that the blood and water which flowed from the wound was a sure sign that life was not extinct.

Conversing thus, we arrived at the grotto, Joseph and Nicodemus going before. We were, in all, twenty-four brethren of the first degree.

Entering, we perceived the white robed novice kneeling upon the moss strewn floor of the grotto, supporting the head of the revived Jesus on his breast.

And as Jesus recognized his Essene friends, his eyes sparkled with joy; his cheeks were tinted with a faint red, and he sat up, asking: 'Where am I?'

Then Joseph embraced him, folding him in his arms, told him how it had all come to pass, and how he was saved from actual death by a profound fainting fit, which the soldiers on Calvary though was death.

And Jesus wondered, and felt on himself; and praising God, he wept on the breast of Joseph. Then Nicodemus urged his friends to take some refreshments, and he ate some dates and some bread dipped in honey. And Nicodemus gave wine to drink, after which Jesus was greatly refreshed, so that he raised himself up.

Then it was that he became conscious of the wounds in his hands and in side. But the balsam which Nicodemus had spread upon them had a soothing effect, and they had already commence to heal.

After the 'byssus' wrappings had been taken off and the muckender was removed from his head, Joseph spoke and said: 'This is not a place in which to remain longer, for here the enemies might easily discover our secret, and betray us.'

After the Sabbath had past, upon the first day of the week, before sunrise, Mary Magdalene, Mary – his mother, along with Salome and Joanna, together with other women, came towards the sepulcher bringing the sweet spices which they had brought and prepare in order to annoint him. The women, after arriving at the sepulcher, met a young Essene novice (the same one who had rolled the stone away); he told the woman:

"Fear not, for I know you seek Jesus who was crucified. He is not here; he is risen as he said. Come, see Jesus the place where the Lord lay."

They entered the sepulcher but did not find the body of Prophet Jesus; they were greatly perplexed about this. Then they saw another young man, sitting on the right side of clothed in a long white garment. They were afraid and bowed down their faces to the earth, and the two spoke to them:

"Why seek you the living among the dead? He is not here but is risen:

Remember how he spoke to your when he was yet in Galilee, saying, "The Son of Man must be delivered into the hands sinful men, and be crucified, and the third day rise again. 'Go quickly on your way; tell his disciples and Peter that he goes before you into Galilee; there you shall see him as he said to you."

At this point in time, it is alleged, in the Gospel's of Matthew and Mark, the following:

"Then he appeared first to Mary Magdalene, and to his Mother Mary, also the mother of James and Joses. Jesus greeted them, saying, All hail!"

Then they came, and held him by his feet, they also showered him with reverence. Jesus said to them, Be not afraid, Go and tell my brothers that they proceed to Galilee, and there they shall see me.

Mary Magdalene went and told them who had been with him as they mourned and wept. They, when they had heard that he was alive and had been seen by her, did not believe. Eventually, the other woman told these matters to the Apostles. However, their words deemed to them as idle tales, and they did not believe them.

Then Peter arose and ran to the sepulchre; stooping down, he beheld the linen cloths lying by themselves, and he departed wondering to himself at what had come to pass.

Jesus was not yet strong enough to walk far, wherefore he was conducted to the house belonging to our Order, that is close by Calvary, in the garden, which also belongs to our brethren.

Another young Brother of our Order was dispatched at once to assist the novice who had been watching by the grave of Jesus, to annihilate every trace of the byssus wrappings and the medicines and drugs using.

When Jesus arrived at the house of our brethren he was faint and weak. His wounds had began to cause him pain. He was moved in that he considered it all a miracle.

'God has let me rise', he said, 'that he may prove in me that which I have taught, and I will slow my disciples that I do live.'

After leaving the sepulcher, Jesus is known to have been seen by many of his disciples at different times. Even when some of his disciples were taken by surprise and disbelief, Jesus proved to them that he was the same person who was put on the cross and not a ghost. He seemed (at that point in time), to have been moving away from Jerusalem in the direction of Galilee.

He avoided public contact intentionally. As he sat upon his journey, he met two disciples, who were going to a village named Emmaus, about eleven kilometers from Jerusalem.

They didn't recognize him at first;

Then he said to them, "O fools and slow of heart to believe all that the Prophets have spoken: Ought not Christ to have suffered these things and to enter into his glory?33

He did not want to go into the village for fear of being recognised.

On another occasion he met some disciples:

And as they thus spoke, Jesus himself stood in the midst and said to them,

"Peace be unto you. They were terrified and affrighted, and supposed that they had seen a spirit. He upbraided them for their unbelief and hardness of hearth because they did not believe them who had seen after he had risen. Why are you troubled? Why do thoughts arise in your hearts? Look at my hands and my feet; it is I, myself: handle me and see, for a spirit has no flesh and bones as you see me have.

When he had thus spoken, he showed them his hands and his feet. While they yet did not believe for joy and wonderment, he said to them Have you here any meat? They gave him a piece of a broiled fish and of a honeycomb, and he took it, and did eat before them.

Then he said to them, these are the words which I spoke to you, while I was yet with you, that all things must be filled which were written in the Law of Moses, and in the Prophets, and in the Psalms concerning me.

He opened their understanding that they might comprehend the scriptures, and he said to them, Thus, it is written, and thus, it behove the Messiah to suffer and to rise from the dead the third day."34

The Gospel of John, Chapter 20 Verses 25; tells us that, when Thomas one of his disciples, learnt of Jesus was alive and well, he said:

"Except I shall see in his hands the print of the nails, and put my finger into the prints of the nails, and thrust my hand into his side, I will not believe."

Eight days later, he met Jesus along with the other disciples.

Jesus showed him where the nail marks were and told Thomas to thrust his finger into the place where the scar was located, and also into his side, so as to see for himself that he was alive with the same body and not a ghost.

Thus, the prophecy that Jesus made was proved to the fullest, just as Jonah entered the whale's body alive, remained in it alive though unconscious, and came out of it alive, so-too did Jesus, entered the tomb alive, remained alive, though unconscious and came out alive.

At this juncture, the following should be noted from Professor S.G.G. Brandon and his book:

The Trial of Jesus of Nazareth; Chapter 07 – 'Trial of Jesus in Early Christian Tradition and Art':

"The Centurion, having witnessed the death of Jesus and the attendant omens, reported to Pilate and his wife what had happened. They are greatly affected by the news, and abstain from food that day.

The tendency is still further developed in another Greek text, which takes the form of a report by Pilate to the Emperor Tiberius about the crucifixion of Jesus and his resurrection.

Pilate puts the blames on the Jews and on Herod, Archelaus, Philip, Annas and Caiaphas – obviously a list of Jewish magnates, called carelessly from the Gospels of Matthew and Luke.

On receiving the letter, the Emperor is enraged with Pilate and orders his arrest and transport to Rome, and the Jews are enslaved for their wickedness.

Pilate is beheaded, but he dies piously.

It also goes on to state:

Procla, the wife of Pilate was canonised as a Saint in the Eastern Church and Pilate achieved this distinction among the Ethopian Christians."

Another interested piece of factual information, is a second alleged letter, that Pontius Pilate sent to Emperor Claudius (Roman Emperor from 41 AD – 54 AD). The letter is in the form of a report, which can be found in the Greed Acts of Peter and Paul and as an appendix to the Gospel of Nicodemus in Latin. This translation of this report is from M.R. James as given in Quasten's Patrology, Volume Ol. Page 117.

The Report of Pontius Pilate to Emperor Claudius, as follows:

Pontius Pilate unto Claudius, greetings.

There befell of late a matter which I myself brought to light (or, made trial of): for the Jews through envy have punished themselves and their posterity with fearful judgement of their own fault; for where as their fathers had promised (al. had announced unto them) that their God would send them out of heaven his holy one who should of right be called their king, and did promise that he would send him upon earth by a virgin; he then (or this God of the Hebrews, then) came when I was governor of Judea, and they beheld him enlightening the blind, cleansing lepers, healing the palsied, driving devils out of men, raising the dead, rebuking the winds, walking upon the waves of the sea dry-shod, and doing many other wonders, and all the people of the Jews calling him the Son of God: the chief priests therefore, moved with envy against him, took him and delivered him unto me and brought against him one false accusation after another, saying that he was a sorcerer and did things contrary to law.

But I, believing that these things were so, having scourged him, delivered him unto their will:

and they crucified him, and when he was buried they set guards upon him. But while my soldiers watched him he rose again on the third day: yet so much was the malice of the Jews kindled that they gave money to the soldiers, saying: Say ye that his disciples stole away his body. But they, pass for they also have testified that they saw him arisen and that they received money from the Jews. And these things have I reported (unto thy mightiness) for this cause, lest some other should lie unto thee (Lat. lest any lie otherwise) and though shouldest deem right to believe the false tales of the Jews.

As Jesus was anxious to see, and to have met his disciples and prove that he was still alive, members of the Essene sect advised him to live in seclusion for the shake of his safety and thus remain "dead to the world."

"Thou are not safe this country, for they will search after thee. Do not, live among thy friends forever,and thy disciples will publish it to the world. Remain, I pray thee, dead to the world. The Brotherhood has brought thee back to life through its secrets, therefore live henceforth for our holy Order to which thou art bound. Live in seclusion of wisdom and virtue, unknown to the world."

The Crucifixion by an Eyewitness, goes on to state the following:

"And the brethren warned Jesus of his danger, that he might avoid his enemies and thus fulfill his mission. For they had been secretly informed that Caiaphas intended quietly to arrest and assassinate Jesus, in that he believed him to be a deceiver."

On Jesus' bidding farewell to his disciples on Mount Olive, 'The Crucifixion by an Eyewitness tells us the following:

"And Jesus led them to the place most dear to him, near the summit of Mount Olive, where can be seen almost the whole of the land of Palestine; for Jesus longed once more to look upon the country where he had lived and worked. To the east where seen Jordan, the Dead Sea, and the Arabian Mountains; and to the west shone the fires from the Temple Rock; but on the other side of the mountain where Bethania.

And the chosen disciples believed that Jesus would lead them to Bethania.

But the elders of the Brotherhood has silently come together on the other side of the mountain, ready to travel, waiting with Jesus, as had been agreed upon.

And he exhorted his disciples to be of good cheer, and firm in their faith.

As he spoke, his voice grew more and more melancholy, and his mind was absorbed in solemn transport.

He prayed for the friends he was about to leave, and lifting his arms he blessed them. And the mist rose around the mountain, tinted by the descending sun.

as the disciples knelt down, their faces bent towards the ground, Jesus rose and hastily went away through the gathering mist. When the disciples rose, there stood before them two of our brethren in the white garb of the Brotherhood, and they instructed them not to wait for Jesus, as he was gone, whereupon they hastened away down the mountain.

But in the city there arose a rumour that Jesus was taken up in a cloud, and had gone to heaven. This was invented by the people who had not been present when Jesus departed. The disciples did not contradict this rumour, inasmuch as it served to strengthen their doctrine, and influenced the people who wanted a miracle in order to believe in him."

in the days that followed, Prophet Jesus prepared for an historic sojourn, a journey that would take him to the East in search of the Lost Israelite Tribes.

CHAPTER 06

Migration To The Eastern Countries

The modern era of Literature, especially in the sphere of Comparative Religion and its History, has produced two (2) outstanding investigative personalities and authors in, Professor Fida Hassnain and Mrs. Suzanne Olsson, the former, I would be referring too; due to the fact that ten (10) pieces of extraordinary historical documents was mentioned in his book;

'The Fifth Gospel: Jesus in the East.'

I would also be mentioning the ten pieces, that Professor hassnain mentioned in his book.

The latter, I wish to thank, for her invaluable and priceless advice, and who also mentioned those ten (10) historical documents in her book; 'Jesus in Kashmir, The Lost Tomb.'

Coincidentally, both Professor Hassnain and Mrs. Olsson co-wrote the book;

'Roza Bal, The Tomb of Jesus.'

Our historical journey continues, when Professor Hassnain in his book (which is mentioned above), the following:

"We're informed by the Gospel of Philip, that having been saved from crucifixion, Jesus Christ was nursed by his friends and disciples and remained in hiding for some time. During this period, he imparted special knowledge to Peter and James. After having remained with them for a period of about a year and a half, he made up his mind to leave them. He appointed James as his successor and migrated."

During Prophet Jesus' mission to the Israelites, he declared to them the following:

"And other sheep have I, which are not of this fold: them also must I bring, Israel, and their coming into being as righteous servants of Allah, as well as some history. I mentioned in the Preface, how the ten (10) tribes of Israel were scattered into the wilderness. It is these said ten that the Messiah, Jesus Christ went in search of.

The 'missing years', tells us that Jesus found them, and now in his second (2nd.) journey, he was returning, for a permanent stay. His first visit though, Syria and his confrontation with Saul.

The following is mentioned in the New Testament;

1. And Saul, yet breathing out threatenings and slaughter against the disciples of the Lord, went unto the high priest,

2. And desired of him letters to Damascus to the synagogues that if he found any of this way, whether they were men or women, he might bring them bound unto Jerusalem.

3. And as he journeyed, he came near Damascus: and suddenly there shined round about him a light from heaven:

4. And he fell to the earth, and heard a voice saying unto him, Saul, Saul, why persecutest thou me?

5. And he said, Who art thou, Lord? And the Lord said, I am Jesus whom thou persuecutest: it is hard for thee to kick against the pricks.

6. And he trembling and astonished said, Lord, what wilt thou have me to do? And the Lord said unto him, Arise, and go into the city, and it shall be told thee what thou must do.

7. And the ment which journeyed with him stood speechless, hearing a voice, but seeing no man.

8. And Saul arose from the earth; and when his eyes were opened, he saw no man: but they led him by the hand, and brought him into Damascus.

9. And he was three days without sight, and neither did eat nor drink.

10. And there was a certain disciple at Damascus, named Ananias; and to him said the Lord in a vision, Ananias. And he said, Behold, I am here, Lord.

11. And the Lord said unto him, Arise, and go into the street which is called Straight, and enquired in the house of Judas of on called Saul, of Tarsus: for, behold, he prayeth,

12. And hath seen in a vision a man named Ananias coming in, and putting his hand on him, that he might receive his sight.

13. Then Ananias answered, Lord, I have heard by many of this man, how much evil he hath done to thy saints at Jerusalem:

14. And here he hath authority from the chief priests to bing all that call on thy name.

15. But the Lord said unto him, Go thy way: for he is a chosen vessel unto me, to bear my name before the Gentiles, and kings, and the children of Israel:

16. For I will shew him how great things he must suffer for my name's sake.

17. And Ananias went his way, and entered into the house; and putting his hands on him said, Brother Saul, the Lord, even Jesus, that appeared unto thee in the way as thou camest, hath sent me, that thou mightest receive thy sight, and be filled with the Holy Ghost.

18. And immediately there fell from his eyes as it had been scales: and he received sight forthwith, and arose, and was baptized.

19. And when he had received meat, he was strengthened. Then was Saul certain days with the disciples which were at Damascus. 4

The Messiah, already been saved, and now on a very strange odyssey, was been guided by Allah, so that he could be saved from further persecution. The Prophet and his mother, although been in Syria, they nevertheless had to migrate from Palestine, and thus departed for a far-off country.

Both mother and son, after leaving Syria, traversed from country to country. Some of his disciples followed him from place to place. During his journey towards the east, the Messiah was accompanied by his mother; Lady Mary, Peter his Apostle and Mary Magdalene.

It was a strange coincident that the successor to Buddah has been called Rahula. When he is separated from his mother, a lady devotee named Magdaliyana acts as a messenger between him and him mother.

The word Rahula may mean: Ruh-Allah or the Spirit of God. The lady messenger-Magdaliyana may refer to Mary Magdalene, the consort of Jesus Christ.

The Tomb of Mary Magdalene, has been located about 6 miles from Kashgar in Cental Asia, near the Tadzhikstan-Kirgizia border.

One (1) very famous historical works, tells us the following:

"Jesus (on whom be peace) was named the Messiah because he was a great traveler. He wore a woollen scarf on his head, and a woolen cloak on his body. He had a stick in has hand; he used to wander from country to country and from city to city. At nightfall he would stay where he was. He ate jungle vegetables, drank jungle water, and went on his travels on foot. His companions in one of his travels, once bought a horse for him; he rode the horse one day but as he could not make any provision for the feeding of the horse, he returned it. Journeying from his country, he arrived at Nasibain, which was at a distance of several hundred miles from his home. With him were a few of his disciples who he sent into the city to preach. In the city, however, there were current wrong and unfounded rumours about Jesus (on whom be peace) and his mother. The governor of the city, therefore, arrested the disciples and then summoned Jesus. Jesus miraculously healed some persons and exhibited other miracles. The King of the territory of Nasibain, therefore, with all his armies and his people, became a follower of his. The legend of the 'coming down of food' contained in Holy Qur'an belongs to the days of his travels."5

The Apostle Thomas was desputised to Parthia and India by Jesus. The Parthia Empire extended from Antioch (Turkey) and Palmyria (Syria) to Kabul (Afghanistan) on one side and from the Caspian sea to the Arabian sea. Prophet Jesus wanted to avoid the limits of the Romans and as such, went to Damascus (Syria) first. From there he went to the city of Nisibis, which had a colony of Jews. The city being a meeting ground of many caravan routes, was full of men of all nations, busy in trade and commerce.

Jesus Christ tried his best to conceal his identity, and it was at this place that he came to be known as YUZ ASAPH.

He wore clothes and a turban of white fleece and carried a rod in his hand. He set a seal of silence on his lips, and began his journey further.

Nisibis lay on the silk route from Syria to Mosul and beyond-towards the east. It should be noted that, the Messiah-Prophet Jesus had travelled to there areas, incognito.

A Hadith of Islam tells us thus:

Reported By Abu Huraira (R.A)

God directed Jesus, 'O Jesus! Move from one place to another'- go from one country to another lest thou shouldst be recognised and persecuted.6

It is related by Josephnus, the following:

'The King of Adabene, sent his son Ezad to stay with with Abennerigos, the King of Spasinou Charax at the head of the Persian Gulf. The small principality of Adiabene existed between Tabriz and Mosul, on the banks of the Tigris river. Ezad returned hime to ascend the throne of Adiabene on the death of his father. It was Ananias who had converted Ezad and his queens.

After some years, the King of Parthis accorded him to rule Nisibis with the result that his kingdom would extend right up to the banks of the Mediterranean.

Another historical document, tells us, the following:

"In the days of Hazrat Isa (Jesus), when leapers were cured by him, they, on being admitted among the healthy people, were known as Asaph, Thus Hazrat Isa, who cured leapers also came to be known as Yuz Asaph, for he not only cured them but gathered them under his merciful protection."7

another Hadith of Islam tells us the following:

'Jesus always used to travel; he went from one country to another, and at nightfall whereever he was, he used to eat the vegetation of the jungle and to drink pure water.'8

Jesus Christ, we're told, moved towards the east and reached Babylon, which was on the banks of the Eupheates. From Babylon, Jesus journeyed to Ur and from that place to Kharax, which ships brought the products of India and the far east. From that place, the goods were transported up the Euphrates river to Babylon, then to Arbel in Adiabene and thence to Nisibis and Edessa in the west.

The Lisan-ul-Arab tells us the following on page 461;

'Jesus was named the 'Messiah', because he wandered about, and because he did not stay at one place.'(see JESUS IN INDIA by Hazrat Mirza Ghulam Ahmad – page 67).

Jesus Christ, The Messiah, was known in Persia as Yuz Asaph. His sayings and teachings in the region, as recorded in the Iranian traditions are the same as those of Jesus Christ. This shows that his preachings were popular among the Persians. It is clear that after the advent of Islam, the Christians, the Jews and the Zoroastrians lost importance, and were reduced in numbers. Nevertheless, the sayings and the parables of Jesus Christ in continued in their traditions and lived afterwards as those of YUZ ASAPH.

Jesus Christ delivered many sermons in Persia, and he was welcomed by the people, who listened to him devoutly. The high priest got him arrested, and he was asked about which new God he was speaking to the people about when Zoroaster only had the privileged of communion with the Supreme Being. He was also told that the laws were given to Zoroaster by God, and he should not sow doubts in the heart of believers. On hearing this, Jesus said unto them thus:

It is not of a new God that I speak:
But of our Heavenly Father,
Who has existed since all time;
And who will still be after,
The end of all things.
It is of Him,
That I have discoursed to the people,
Who, Like unto innocent children,
Are not yet capable,
Of comprehending God,
By the simple strength of their intelligence:
Or of Penetrating,
Into his divine,
And spiritual sublimity.

The Messiah, Jesus Christ, told them that he spoke in the name of that heavenly Father. He explained that just as a baby discovers in the darkness its mother's breast; in the same way, people who have been led into error by erroneous doctrine, do recognise by instinct their Heavenly Father. Prophet Jesus, paused a while in many a hamlet, town and cities in Persia.

He preached and healed among the common people, who followed him in throngs.

He even attended a feast in Persepolis.

During his short sojourn in Persia, Jesus sat in silence in the prayer hall of the Magi priests, for seven days. Then he spoke on the origin of evil and good.

He told them not to worship the sun, for it was part of the cosmos which God has created for humanity. It is to God and to God alone, that we owe all that we posses in this world. On hearing him, the priests asked how could a people live according to the rules of justice if it had no preceptor?

Jesus replied that so long as the people had no priests, the natural law governed them, and they preserved the candour of their souls.

He further explained that when their souls were with God, they could commune with the Father, without the medium of any idol or animal or the Sun or the fire.

Professor Fida Hasnain and Mrs. Suzanne Olsson, in their research and quest of the Geography and Topography of where Prophet Jesus went after the events of the Cross; declared that the Messiah and his Companions went towards the east in their onward journey after leaving Persia.

Maybe they visited Hamadan and Nishapur, from which city there are two roads, one leading into Afghanistan via heart and thence to Khandahar and the other leading to Bukhara and Samarkand.

My dear readers, lets take the 'former' road, that leads into Afghanistan.

In the book, 'Among the Dervishes', by O.M. Burke and published by Octagon Press Ltd. (U.K), states in Chapter Eight (8), the following:

'The followers of Isa, son of Maryam-Jesus the son of Mary – generally call themselves Muslims and inhabit a number of villagers scattered throughout the Western area of Afghanistan whose centre is heart.

Their chief is Abba Yahiyya (Father John), who can recite the succession of teachers through sixty generations to – Isa, son of Mary, of 'Nazara', the Kashmiri. According to these people, Jesus escaped from the cross, was hidden by friends, where helped to flee to India, where he had been before during his youth, and settled in Kashmir, where he is revered as an ancient teacher, Yuz Asaf.'

Afghanistan was home to some of the Lost Tribes of Israel and/or sub tribes of Israel. In 2006, there was only two (2) surviving members of the Lost Tribes of Israel.

But another question beckons, where is Afghanistan geographically located?

It is a land locked mountainous country, surrounded by the countries of; Pakistan, Tadzhikstan, Uzbekistan, Turkmenistan and Iran.

It's countryside has plains in the North and Southwest. The highest point in this country is 7485m (24557ft.) above sea level.

Large parts of the country are dry, and fresh water supplies are limited.

The country has a continental climate with hot summers and cold winters.

The country is also frequented by earthquakes.

One point to be noted, is that if the Afghans are part of Bani-Israel, then they are certainly from the progeny of Jacob and the Tribes of Yahuda and Bin Yamin.

A Hadith of Islam tells us the following:

Reported by Abdullah bin Umar (R.A)

'The Holy Prophet (u.w.b.p) declared that the most favoured in the sight of God are the poor. Asked, what was meant by the poor? Where they the people who, like Jesus the Messiah, fled from their country with their faith?9

In another document, the 'Siraj-ul-Maluk', by Ibn-al-Walid Al-Fahri Al-Tartooshi Al-Maliki an dpublished by the Matba Khairiya of Egypt in 1306 A.H. It states on page 6 of his book, the following;

'Where is Isa, the Ruhullah, and the Kalimatullah, who was dead, and that, even a great man like him had departed from this world.

It should be noticed that this learned authority calls Jesus not merely 'traveller' but the 'Chief of travellers.' (see Jesus in India by Mirza Ghulam Ahmad – page 67.)

The sojourn of Prophet Jesus in Afghanistan after the events of the Crucifixion, is still shrouded in a mystery. However the following ancient books, of which many Scholars will know, may offer some insight, into why Prophet Jesus visited Afghanistan-a second time. They are:

1. The Races of Afghanistan by H.W. Bellews C.S.I..

2. Tabaqat-i-Nasri

3. A Narrative of a Visit to Ghazni, Kabul and Afghanistan by G.T. Vigne

4. History of Afghanistan by Col.G.B.Malleson

5. History of the Afghans by L.P Ferrier, translated by Capt.W.M. Jasse

6. Makhzan-i-Afghani by Khawaja Nimatullah of heart, translated and published by Prof.Bernhard Doran of Kharqui University.

There are many more books, but I mentioned these because these books are named in Hazrat

Mirza Ghulam Ahmad's aforementioned book.

The journey continues...........

JESUS IN INDIA AND KASHMIR.

After leaving Afghanistan, Jesus Christ came to the Punjab with the ultimate intention of going to Kashmir after seeing the Punjab and Hindustan (Pakistan and India); it should be noticed that the town or village of Chitral, is a part of the Swat Valley of Pakistan's Punjab region.

If one travels from Afghanistan to Kashmir through the Swat Valley, one has to journey over a distance of 80 miles or about 135 kilometers.

Jesus, however, wisely adopted the route through Afghanistan, so that the lost tribe of Israel, known as Afghans, may profit from has teachings.

The eastern frontier of Kashmir touches Tibet. From Kashmir he could easily go to Tibet. Having come to the Punjab, he had no difficulty in wandering through the important places in both Pakistan and India, before going to Kashmir or Tibet. It is, therefore, quite possible, as some old historical records of this country show, that Jesus may have seen Nepal, Benares and other places to the eastern boundaries of India.

It should be mentioned here, that he stayed in these two (?) territories only through the winter, and by the end of March or the beginning of April returned to Kashmir. As Kashmir resembles Syria and her surrounding country; Prophet Issa must have taken up permanent residence in Kashmir.

It is possible, moreover, that he may have stayed for some time n Afghanistan and it is not impossible that he may have married in that country for one of the tribes of Afghans is known as 'Isa Khel' – it would not be suprising if they are descendants of Jesus.

Before Prophet Jesus left Pakistan, his mother Lady Mary died in about 49 A.D. At a place called Mari then and now called Murree, which is coincidentally a hill station.

In 1898, an engineer had wished to demolish the tomb at the time of the construction of the defence tower; shortly afterwards he died in an accident, and the locals connect the incident with his evil intentions towards the tomb. The grave, which is still facing east, was later repaired.

The valley of Kashmir has been described as paradise on earth by many famous writers!!! The people or this beautiful land call themselves as Kushur. It is also claimed that many tribes settled in this valley during perhistoric times and prominent amongst these were the Kassites or Kush tribe, who founded habitations with the name Kush, such as Kashan in Iran and Hindo-Kush in Afghanistan. This tribe belonged to the sons of Cush, who were ordered to migrate to the land of fat pastures.

The Kashmiris are of a tall, robust frame of body, with manly features; the women are full formed and handsome with aquiline noses and features resembling the Jews. Their physical and ethnic character has always struck being the Jews. Their physical and ethnic character has always struck observant visitors to the valley and they have universally connected them with the Jews. This is the very said place, whose people accepted Jesus with the Jews. This is the very said place, whose people accepted Jesus Christ of Nazareth, who proclaimed his prophethood and his Ministry in this valley, in the year 78 A.D. (3154-Laukika Era) – the year of his arrival.

In the book, Tarikh-i-Kashmir, by historian Mullah Nadri; a mention of Yuz Asaph is made about his stay in Kashmir:

"After him his son Raja Akh (whose name was Ach), came to the throne.

He ruled for sixty years. It is said that he founded the village of Achabaal in Kothar district. After him his son, Gopananda, took the reigns of Government and ruled the country under the name of Gopadtta. During his reign many temples were built and on top of Mount Solomon the dome of the temple became cracked. He deputed one of his ministers named Sulaiman, who had come from Persia to repair it. 'Hindus' objected that he (the Minister) was an infidel (and belonged to) another religion.

"During this time Hazrat Yuz Asaf having come from Bait-ul Maqaddas (the Holy Land) to this holy valley proclaimed his prophethood.

He devoted himself, day and night, in prayers to God, and having attained the neights of piety and virtue, he declared himself to be a Messanger of God for the people of Kashmir. He invited people to his religion.

Because the people of the valley had faith in this Prophet, Raja Gopadatta referred the objection of the

Hindus' to him, for a decision.

It was because of this Prophet's orders that Sulaiman, whom Hindus called Sandeman, completed the repairs to the dome.

The year was Fifty and four (54).

Further, on one of the stones of the stairs, Sulaiman insribed:

'In these times Yuz Asaf proclaimed his prophethood,' and on the other stone of the stairs he also insribed that he (Yuz Asaph) was Yusu, Prophet of the Children of Israel.'

Jesus had declared, that he was, 'The Messenger of the Messiah', but the Jews had refected him, instead they considered themselves as the chosen nation and their God as the one God of Israel only.

Jesus believed and preached universal brotherhood; including prophesying the advent of Islam's holy Prophet, to whom he declared was the 'White Cloud of Mercy.' The Jews declared even further that the (Jesus/Issa) was a dissident and they attempted to have him crucified, but he survived and after a number of years (45?), journeyed to Kashmir; where a large number of the Lost Tribes of Israel can be found.

The folliong is the English translation of the information displayed on the signpost that stands outside the Tomb of Jesus in Srinagar, Kashmir; it is taken from the Tarikh-i-Azam by Khwaja Azam Deddmari:

"Nearby is situated the stone of the grave which, according to the people, is the Prophet's who arrived from a far off place during ancient times.

Anointed for Kashmir: This spot is famous as the resting place of a messenger.

Also recorded in the History books of India and Iran, two (2) meetings between Prophet Issa and King Shalivahana; one of their meetings is as follows:

"Shalivahana, who was a grandson of Bikram Jit, took over the government. He vanquished the attacking hordes of Chinese, Parthians, Scythians and Bactrians. He drew a border between the Aryians and the Maleacha (non-Aryians), and ordered the latter to withdraw to the other side of India. There, in the land of the Hun (Ladakh, a part of the Kushan empire), the powerful king saw a man sitting on a mountain, who seemed to promise auspiciousness. His skin was fair and he wore white garments.

The king asked the holy man who he was. The other replied: 'I am called a son of God, born of a virgin, minister of the non-believers, relentless in search of the truth. 'The king, I come from a foreign country, where there is no longer truth and where evil knows no bounds. In the land of the non-believers, I appeared as the Messiah. But the demon Ihamasi of the barbarians (dasyu) manifested herself in a terrible form; I was delievered unto her in manner of the non-believers and ended in Ihamasi's realm."

The above mentioned extraction was taken from the ninth book of the Hindus entitled, The Bhavishya Mahapurana, which was complied by Sutta in the year 3191 of the Kaukikai Era. That corresponds to the year 115 AD.

in the second meeting, which occurred not to long after (probable a few months thereafter): It is recorded in an old Persian book entitled the Negaris-Tan-I-Kashimr, that relates to King Shalivahan (the same king who met and conversed with Nabi-Issa in the mountains), who told Jesus that he needed a woman to take care of him, and offered his choice of fifty. Jesus replied that he did not need any and that no one was obliged to work for him, but the king persisted until Jesus agreed to employ a women to cook for him, look after his house and do his washing.

The woman's name was Maryan, and according to the said book she bore Jesus children.

Sadly enough, Prophet of the Lost Sheep of Israel, who settled down preached and got married died at the age of 120 of the said year of 120 A.D. The day he died is unknown, but when he passed away, it was a great period of mourning for the Kashmiris of that era. According to Jewish customs, the body of dead had to remain on the shelf, and after decomposition, the bones would be stored in a wooden or stone chest; nevertheless the sacred body of Jesus or Yuz Asaph, as he was known as, was laid in a sepulchre, according to the Jewish style.

A large tomb was later erected on his grave and it eventually became a place of pilgrimage for all, whether rich or poor. People came with offerings at the tomb and led prayers there. Thomas his brother, who had always devoted his life to the services of Jesus, his brother and Prophet of God. Thomas felt very much bereaved and left for Malabar to preach among the lost tribes there. Thomas preached amongst the people of south India and established seven churches there. He suffered martyrdom at Maelapur in Madras (Chennai) and is buried there.

The Tomb of Yuz Asaph is located in Anzimar, Khanyar, Srinager, the summer capital of Kashmir. Srinagar, which means the city of the sun, is an ancient city. It is divided into two parts, the old and the new city.

The tomb is located in the old city.

At this juncture, it is mentioned in the Ain-ul-Havat: Volume 2, Chapter 2, pages 177 to 178 by author Ibn-i-Muhammed Hadi Muhammed Ismail regarding Yuz Asaph viz:

"He went to many cities and preached to those cities. At last he reached the city of Kashmir. He invited its inhabitants to righteousness and resided there till death approachd him, and his holy spirit departed from his earthly body and went to rest with God. But before his death he called his companion Ba'bad and made a will... and directed him to construct a tomb for him. He laid himself with his head towards the East and stretched his legs towards the West, and went to the place of Eternity."

The present building built from bricks and mortar is raised on the ancient stone sepulcher. The building is in reality a rectangular structure enclosed by walls made of chiselled stone blocks of a big size.

Very recently, the ancient stone walls have been plastered with cement, but the upper portion of the original door for access to the crypt is still visible. Its decorated stones have been plastered with cement.

The cellar is an ancient structure decorated internally but access to it has been blocked by a road on the west side which was built some time ago. This particular cellar is the original sepulcher containing the remains of Yuz Asaph a.k.a Jesus of Nazareth. The structure above it contains the following:

1. Outer wooden sarcophagus.

2. Inner wooden sarcophagus.

3. Two artificial gravestones.

4. One stone slab with carved foot prints.

5. One rectangular stone slab or gravestones.

6. One wooden cross.

7. One wooden incense stand.

8. This tomb was built in the Jewish style, with a room underground and having a side door. Near the grave is a stone slab engraved with footprints bearing traces of crucifixion marks; one foot impression has a small round hole and the other has a raised scar wound. These footprints were carved by some ancient and unknown artist. As they represent crucifixion marks, it is possible that whoever carved them might have seen Jesus in person.

The most interesting information comes from the followers of Issa, Son of Miriam, who call themselves Moslems; they once a week, join in a ritual meal in which bread and wine are taken as symbolic of the grosser and finer nutritions which are the experiences of attainment of nearness to Allah. They are convinced too, that the day will come when the world will discover the truth about Jesus.

To conclude, this is what India's former Prime Minister, the late Pundit Jawahar Lal Nehru said in his book; <u>Glimpses of World History</u>:-

"All over central Asia, in Kashmir had Laddakh and Tibet and even further North, there is still a strong belief that Jesus of Isa travelled about there.

I am confident, therefore, that when those who are endowed with the gift of reason and wisdom will think sincerely, keeping in mind that Jesus came out from sepulcher alive with his wounded moral body and did not ascend to heaven but lived on earth will come to the conclusion that the entombed person in Khan Yar Street (Srinagar, Kashmir) is Jesus the Son of Mary (peace be upon him).

This is our answer to all those who may ask us. If Jesus did not die upon the Cross, where did he go and where did he die?

In this lies the solution of the complicated question about the unknown life of Jesus. If anyone can produce any other solution more credible and reasonable than this, let him come forward and produce it and the world will judge for itself.

Finally I would like to say that were the archaeologists to open the tomb and explore it, they might find some epitaphs upon the stones or other signs in support of the aforesaid discovery, and thus they might redeem hundreds of millions of their fellow-beings from worshipping a man who was sent to call the people to the worship of the one had only GOD." (page 84)

Chapter 07

Paraclete

The word Paraclete comes from the Greek word – Parakletos, which means, "one who consoles-a comforter", or "one who intercedes on our behalf-an advocate."

The Bible tells us thus:

"And I will pray the Father, and he shall give you another Comforter, that he may abide with you for ever."1

also,

"There things have I spoken unto you, being yet present with you. But the Comforter, which is the Holy Ghost, whom the Father will send in my name, he shall teach you all things, and bring all things to your remembrance, whatsoever I have said unto you."2

And also,

"But when the Comforter is come, whom I will send unto you from the Father, even the Spirit of truth, which proceedeth from the Father, he shall testify of me."3

In other place, the Bible tells us;

"Nevertheless I tell you the truth; It is expedient for you that I go away: for I go not away, the Comforter will not come, he will reprove the world of sin, and, and of righteousness, and of judgment."4

And also,

"I have yet many things to say unto you, but ye cannot bear them now. However when he, the Spirit of truth is come, he will guide you into all truth: for he shall not speak of himself; but whatsoever he shall hear, that shall he speak: and he will show you things to come."5

In another part of the Bible, it tells us thus;

"Behold my servant, whom I have chosen; my beloved, in whom my soul is will pleased: I will put my spirit upon him, and he shall show judgment to the Gentiles.

And in his name shall the Gentiles trust.

Wherefore I say unto you, All manner of sin and blasphemy shall be forgiven unto men: but the blasphemy against the Holy Ghost shall not be forgiven unto men. And whosoever speaketh a word against the Son of man, it shall be forgiven him, but whosoever speaketh against the Holy Ghost, it shall not be forgiven him, neither in this world, neither in the world to come."6

The person spoken of in the above Biblical references, is no lesser person than the son of Hazrat Abdullah and Lady Aminah, and is the Seal of Prophethood. He is Islam's Holy Prophet Muhammed (u.w.b.p) – 570 AD to 632 AD. To my Christian and Jewish friends, I know what you'll might be thinking, but, please remember the words of the Prophet Jesus, when he said;

"There I say unto you, The Kingdom of God shall be taken from you, and given to a nation bringing forth the fruits thereof."7

The Old Testament tells us;

"I will raise them up a Prophet from their brethren, like unto thee, and will put my words in his mouth; and he shall speak unto them all that I shall command him."8

Prophet Jesus was the last of the Israelite prophets, of whom I dealt with, earlier in this book. As you would be aware, this Chapter, deals the last of the Ishmaelite prophets', once again, his name being Muhammed or Ahamad (u.w.b.p). A very famous Qur'anic passage, tells us thus;

"And when Jesus, son of Mary said: O Children of Israel, surely I am the messenger of Allah to you, verifying that which is before me of the Toran and giving the good news of a Meaaenger who will come after me, his name being Ahamad. But when he came to them with clear arguments, they said:

This is clear enchantment."9

The Prophet of Islam's lineage, can be traced back to the seed of the Prophet Ishmael and his father, Prophet Abraham. For those who have forgotton what Allah has said, the Old Testament tells us thus;

"And as for Ishmael, I have heard thee: Behold, I have blessed him, and will make him fruitful, and will multiply him exceedingly; twelve princes shall he beget, and I will make him a great nation."10

also,

"Arise, lift up the lad, and hold him in thine hand; for I will make him a great nation. And he dwelt in the wilderness of Paran: and his mother took him a wife out of the land of Egypt."11

The Holy Qur'an tells us, thus;

"Our Lord, I have settled a part of my offspring in a valley unproductive of fruit near Thy Sacred House, our Lord, that they may keep up prayer; so make the hearts of some people yearn towards them, and provide them with fruits; haply they may be grateful."12

The Old Testament tells us the following'

"These are their generations; The first-born of Ishmael; Bebaioth, Kedar, Abdeel, Mibsam, Mishma, Dumar, Massa, Hadad, Tema, Jetur, Naphish and Kademah."13

The above religious references, speaks for themselves, I need not say anything further, with regards to Prophet Ishmael.

Prophet Muhammed (u.w.b.p) was born in Mecca, Saudi Arabia in the year 570 AD. His birth was foretold thus;

"Therefore the Lord himself shall call his name Immanuel.

Butter and honey shall he eat, that he may know to refuse the evil, and choose the good."14

The usual staple food of the Holy Prophet of Islam, consisted of dates, barley bread and milk. Abu Dawood records that the Holy Prophet used to take delight in eating butter and Sahih Bukhari records a similar Hadith regarding honey.

Prophet Muhammed's office of prophethood was prophesied in the Old Testament as follows;

"I charge you, O daughters of Jerusalem, if ye find my beloved, that ye tell him, that I am sick of love. What is thy beloved more than another beloved, O thou fairest among women? What is thy beloved more than another beloved, that thou does so charge us? My beloved is white and ruddy, the chiefest among ten thousand. His head is as the most fine gold, his locks are bushy, and black as a raven. His eyes are as the eyes of doves by the river of waters, washed with milk, and fitly set.

His cheeks are as a bed of spices, as sweet flowers: his lips like lilies, dropping sweet smelling myrrh. His hands are as gold rings set with the beryl: his belly is as bright ivory overlaid with sapphires. His legs are as pillars of marble, set upon sockets of fine gold: his countenance is as Lebanon, excellent as the cedars.

His mouth is most sweet: yea, he is altogether lovely. This is my beloved, and this is my friend, O daughters of Jerusalem."15

We're further told in the Old Testament, the following;

"Moreover concerning the stranger, which is not of thy people Israel, but is come from a far country for thy great name's sake, and thy mighty hand, and thy stretched out arm; if they come and pray in this house; then hear thou from the heavens, even from thy dwelling place, and do according to all that the stranger calleth to thee for; that all people of Israel, and may know that this house which I have built is called by thy name."16

9.   The religion of the Paraclete, is foretold thus;

"Sing unto the Lord, a new song, and his praise from the end of the earth, ye that go down to the sea, and all that is therein; the isles, and the inhabitants thereof.

Let the wilderness and the cities thereof lift up their voice, the villages that Kedar does inhabit: let the inhabitants of the rock sing, let them shout from the top of the mountain."17

To another place, it tells us thus;

"God came from Teman, and the Holy One from mount Paran. Selah.

His glory covered the heavens, and the earth was full of his praise.

And his brightness was as the light; he had horns coming out of hand: and there was the hiding of his power. Before him went the pestilence, and the burning coals went forth as his feet. He stood, and measured the earth:

He beheld, and drove asunder the nations; and the everlasting.

I saw the tents of Cushan in affliction: and the curtains of the land of Midian did tremble."18

Prophet Muhammed (u.w.b.p), continues to be mentioned in the Old Testament, but in an allegorical language; as thus,

1.   Give the king thy judgments, O God, and thy righteousness unto the king's son.

2.   He shall judge thy people with righteousness, and thy poor with judgment.

3. The mountains shall bring peace to people, and the little hills, by righteousness.

4. He shall judge the poor of the people, he shall save the children of the needy, and shall break in pieces the oppressor.

5. They shall fear thee as long as the sun and moon endure, throughout all generations.

6. He shall come down like rain upon the mown grass: as showers that water the earth.

7. In his days shall the righteous flourish; and abundance of peace so long as the moon endureth.

8. He shall give dominion also from sea to sea, and from the river unto the ends of the earth.

9. They that dwell in the wilderness shall bow before him; and his enemies shall lick the dust.

10. The kings of Tarshish and of the isles shall bring presents: the kings of Sheba and Seba shall offer gifts.

11. Yea, all kings shall fall down before him: all nations shall serve him.

12. For he shall deliver the needy when he crieth; the poor souls of the needy.

13. He shall spare the poor and needy, and shall save the souls of the needy.

14. He shall redeem their soul from deceit and violence: and precious shall their blood be in his sight.

15. And he shall live, and to him shall be given of the gold of Sheba: prayer also shall be made from him continually; and daily shall he be praised.

16. There shall be an handful of corn in the earth upon the top of the mountains; the fruit thereof shall shake like Lebanon: and they of the city shall flourish like grass of the earth.

17. His name shall endure for ever: his name shall be continued as long as the sun: and men shall be blessed in him: all nations shall call him blessed.

18. Blessed be the LORD God, the God of Israel, who doeth wondrous things.

19. And blessed be his glorious name for ever: and let the whole earth be filled with his glory; Amen, and Amen.

20. The prayers of David the son of Jesus are ended. 19

Another place in the Old Testament, also tell us, thus;

1. Arise, shine, for thy light is come, and the glory of the LORD is risen upon thee.

2. For, behold, the darkness shall cover the earth, and gross darkness the people: but the LORD shall arise upon thee, and his glory shall be seen upon thee.

3. And the Gentiles shall come to thy light, and kings to the britghtness of thy rising.

4. Lift up thine eyes around about, and see: all they gather themselves together, they come to thee: thy sons shall come from far, and thy daughters shall be nursed at thy side.

5. Then thou shall see, and flow together, and thine heart shall fear, and be enlarged; because the abundance of the sea shall bring gold and incense; and they shall shew forth the praises of the LORD.

6. The multitude of camels shall cover thee, the dromedaries of Midian and Ephah; all they from Sheba shall come: they shall bring gold and incense, and they shall shew forth the praises of the LORD.

7. All the flocks of Kedar shall be gathered together unto thee, the rams of Nebaioth shall minister unto thee: they shall come up with acceptance on mine altar, and I will glorify the house of my glory.

8. Who are these that fly as a cloud, and as the doves to their windows?

9. Surely the isles shall wait for me, and the ships of Tarshish first, to bring thy sons from far, their silver and their gold with them, unto the name of the LORD thy God, and to the Holy One of Israel, because he hath glorified thee.

10. And the sons of strangers shall build up thy walls, and their kings shall minister unto thee: for in my warth I smote thee, but in my favour have I had mercy on thee.

11. Therefore thy gates shall be open continually; they shall not be shut day nor night; that men may bring unto thee the forces of the Gentiles, and that their kings may be brought.

12. For the nation and kingdom that will not serve thee shall perish; yea, those nations shall be utterly wasted.

13. The glory of Labanon shall come unto thee, the fir tree, the pine tree, and the box together, to beautify the place of my sanctuary; and I will make the place of my feet glorious.

14. The sons also of them that afflicted thee shall come bending unto thee; and all they that despised thee shall bow at the soles of thy feet; and they shall call thee; The city of the LORD, The Zion of the Holy One of Israel.

15. Whereas thou has been forsaken and hated, so that no man went through thee, I will make thee an eternal excellency, a joy of many generations.

16. Thou shalt also suck the milk of the Gentiles, and shalt suck the breast of kings: and thou shalt know that I the LORD am thy Saviour and thy Redeemer, the mighty One of Jacob.

17. For brassi will bring gold, and for iron I will bring silver, and for wood brass, and for stones iron: I will also make thy officers peace, and thine exactors righteousness.

18. Violence shall no more be heard in thy land, wasting nor destruction within thy borders; but thou shalt call thy walls Salvation, and thy gates Praise.

19. Thy sun shall no more go down; neither for brightness shall the moon give light unto thee: but the LORD shall be unto thee an everlasting light, and thy God thy glory.

20. Thy sun shall no more go down; neither shall thy moon withdraw itself: for the LORD shall be thine everlasting light, and the days of thy mourning shall be ended.

21. Thy people also shall be all righteous: thy shall inherit the land for ever, the branch of my planting, the work of my hands, that I may be glorified.

22. A little one shall become a thousand, and a small one a strong nation: I the LORD will hasten it in his time.20

The year is 624AD, Muslims led by Prophet Muhammed (u.w.b.p), defeat the infidels of Mecca, at the wells of Badr aka The Battle of Badr. This Battle is mentioned in the Bible, thus;

"And he saw a chariot with a couple of horsemen, a chariot of asses, and a chariot of camels; and he hearkened diligently with much heed:

the burden upon Arabia. In the forest in Arabia shall ye lodge, O ye travelling companies of Dedanim. The inhabitants of the land of Tema brought water to him that was thirst, they prevented with their bread him that fled. For they fled from the swords, from the drawn sword, and from the bent bow, and from the grievousness of war. For thus hath the Lord said unto me, withing the year, according to the years of an hireling, and all the glory of Kedar shall fail: And the residue of the number of archers, the mighty men of the children of Kedar, shall be diminished: for the Lord God of Israel hath spoken it."21

The Prophet of Islam, Paraclete or The Comforter, is but one (1) person! Prophet Muhammed (u.w.b.p). the world's most respected religious Personality, is conspicuously mentioned in the Gospel of St. Barnabas, approximately -31 times. I shall only mention six (6) places, where his immaculate name is mentioned viz;

Gospel of St. Barnabas
39:Adam Gets Life

Then said John: 'Well hast thou spoken, O master, but we lack to know how man sinned through pride.'

Jesus answered: 'When God has expelled Satan, and the angel Gabriel had purified that mass of earth whereon Satan spat. God created everything that liveth, both of the animals that fly and of them that walk and swim, and he adorned the world with all that it hath. One day Satan approached unto the gates of paradise, and, seeing the horses would be for them grievous labour; and that if the mass of earth should receive a soul there trample that piece of earth in such wise that it should be no more good for anything. The horses aroused themselves and impetuously sat themselves to urn over that piece of earth which lay among lilies and roses.

Whereupon God gave spirit to that unclean portion of earth upon which lay the spittle of Satan, which Gabriel had taken up from the mass; and raise up the dog, who' barking filled the horses with fear, and they fled. Then God gave his soul to man, while all the holy angels sang: 'Blessed be thy holy name, O God our Lord.'

'Adam, having sprung up upon his feet, saw in the air a writing that shone like the sun, which said: "There is only one God, and Mohammed is the messenger of God." Whereupon Adam opened his mouth and said: "I thank thee, O Lord my God , that thou hast designed to create me; but tell me. I pray thee, what meaneth the message of these words: "Mohammed is messenger of God. Have there been other men before me?"

'Then said God: "Be thou welcome, O my servant Adam. I tell thee that thou art the first man whom I have created And he whom thou hast seen [mentioned] is thy son, who shall come into the world many years hence, and shall be my messenger, for whom I have created all things; who shall give light to the world when he shall come; whose soul was set in a celestial splendor sixty thousand years before I made anything."

'Adam besought God, saying: "Lord, grant me this writing upon the nails of the fingers of my hands." Then God gave to the first man upon his thumbs that writing: upon the thumb-nail on the left it said: "Mohammed is messenger of God." Then with fatherly affection the first man kissed those words, and rubbed his eyes, and said: "Blessed be that day when thou shalt come to the world."

'Seeing the man alone, God said: "It is not well that he should remain alone." Wherefore he made him to sleep, and took a rib from near his heart, filling the place with them as lords of Paradise, to whom he said: "Behold I give unto you every fruit to eat, except the apples and the corn" whereof he said: "Beware that in no wise ye eat of these fruits, for ye shall become unclean, insomuch that I shall not suffer you to remain here, but shall drive you forth, and ye shall suffer great miseries."

Gospel of St. Barnabas

54: Of the Judgment Day

'When these signs he passed, there shall be darkness over the world forty years. God alone being alive, to whom be honour and glory for ever. When the forty years be passed. God shall give life to his messenger, who shall rise again like the sun, but resplendent as a thousand suns. He shall sit, and shall not speak, for he shall be as it were beside himself. God shall raise again the four angels favoured of God, who shall seek the messenger of God, and , having found him, shall station themselves on the four side of the place to keep watch upon him. Next shall God give life to all the angels, who shall come like bees circling round the messenger of God. Next shall God give life to all his prophets, who, following Adam, shall go every one to kiss the hand of the messenger of God, committing themselves to his protection. Next shall God give life to all the elect, who shall cry our: "O Mohammed, be mindful of us!" At whose cries pity shall awake in the messenger of God, and he shall consider what he ought to do, fearing for their salvation. Next shall God give life to every created thing, and they shall return their former existence, but every one shall besides possess the power of speech. Next shall God give life to all the reprobates, at whose resurrection, by reason of their hideousness, all the creatures of God shall be afraid, and shall cry: "Let not thy mercy forsake us, O Lord our God." After this shall God cause Satan to be raised up, at whose aspect every creature shall be as dead for, for fear of the horrid form of his appearance. May it please god,' said Jesus, 'that I behold not that monster of that day. The messenger of God alone shall not be affrighted by such shapes, because he shall fear God alone.

'Then the angel, at the sound of whose trumpet all shall be raised, shall sound his trumpet again, saying: "Come to the judgment, O creatures, for your Creator willeth to judge you." Then shall appear in the midst of heaven over the valley of Jehosphaphat a glittering throne, over which shall come a while cloud, whereupon the angels shall cry out:
"Blessed be thou our God shall fear, for that he shall perceive that none hath loved God as he should. For he who would get in change a piece of gold must have sixty mites; wherefore, if he have but one mite he cannot change it. But if the messenger of God shall fear, what shall the ungodly do who are full of wickedness?"
Gospel of St. Barnabas
55: Muhammad at the Judgment Day

'The messenger of God shall go to collect all the prophets, to whom he shall speak, praying them to go with him to pray God for the faithful. And every one shall excuse himself for fear; nor, as God liveth, would I go there, knowing what I know. Then God, seeing this, shall remind his messenger how he created all things for love and reverence, while the angel sing: "Blessed be thy holy name O God, our God."

'And when the hath drawn nigh unto the throne, God shall open [his mind] unto his messenger, even as a friend unto a friend when for a long while they have not met. The first to speak shall be the messenger of God, who shall say: "I adore and love thee, O my God, and with all my heart and soul I give thee thanks for that thou didst vouchsafe to create me to be thy servant, and madest all for love of me, so that I might love thee for all things and in a things created of God shall say: "We give thee thanks, O Lord, and bless thy holy name." Verily I say unto you, the demons and reprobates with satan shall then weep so that more water shall flow from the eyes of one of them than is in the river of Jordan. Yet shall they not see God.

'And God shall speak unto his messenger, saying: "Thou art welcome, O my faithful servant; therefore ask what thou wilt, for thou shalt obtain all." The messenger of God shall answer. "O Lord, I remember that when thou didst create me, thou saidst that thou hadst willed to make for love of me the world and paradise, and angels and men, that they might glorify thee by me thy servant. Therefore, Lord God, merciful and just. I pray thee that thou recollect thy promise made unto thy servant."

'And God shall make answer even as friend who jesteth with a friend, and shall say:
"Hast thou witnesses of this, my friend Mohammed?" And with reverence he shall say:
"Yes, Lord." Then God shall answer: "Go, call them, O Gabriel." The angel Gabriel shall come to the messenger of God shall answer: "They are Adam, Abraham, Ishmael, Moses, David, and Jesus son of Mary."

'Then shall the angel depart, and he shall call the aforesaid witnesses, who with fear shall go thither. And when they are present God shall say unto them: "Remember ye that which my messenger affirmeth?" They shall reply: "What things, O Lord?" God shall say: "That I have made all things for love of him, so that all things might praise me by him." Then every one of them shall answer: "There are with us three witnesses better than we are, O Lord." And God shall reply: "Who are these three witnesses?" Then Moses shall say:

"The book that thou gavest to me is the first"; and David shall say: "The book that thou gavest to me is the second"; and he who speaketh to you shall say: "Lord, the whole world, deceived by Satan, said that I was thy son and thy fellow, but the book that thou gavest me said truly that I am thy servant; and that book confesseth that which thy messenger affirmeth." Then said shall the messenger of God speak, and shall say: "Thus saith the book that thou gaveth me, O Lord." And when the messenger of God hath said this, god shall speak, saying: "All that I have now done, I have done in order that every one should know how much I love thee." And that I have now done, I have done in order that every one should know how much I love thee." And when he hath thus spoken, God shall give unto his messenger a book, in which are written all the names of the elect of God. Wherefore every creature shall do reverence to God, saying "To thee alone, O God, be glory and honour, because thou hast given us to thy messenger."

Gospel of St. Barnabas
96: Mercy to the World

When the prayer was ended, the priest said with a loud voice: Stay Jesus for we need to know who thou art, for the quieting of our nation.'

Jesus answered: 'I am Jesus, son of Mary, of the seed of David, a man that is mortal and feareth God be given honour and glory.'

The priest answered: 'In the book of Moses it is written that our God must said us the Messiah, who shall come to announce to us that which God willeth, and shall bring to the world the mercy of God. Therefore I pray thee tell us the truth, art thou the Messiah of God whom we expert?'

Jesus answered: 'It is true that God hath so promised, but indeed I am not he, for he is made before me, and shall come after me.'

The priest answered 'By thy words and signs at any rate we believe thee to be a prophet and an holy one of God, wherefore I pray thee in the name of a Judaea and Israel that thou for love of god shouldst tell us in what wise the Messiah will come.'

Jesus answered: 'As God liveth,in whose presence my soul standeth, I am not the Messiah whom all the tribes of the earth expect, even as God promised to our father Abraham, saying: "In thy seed will I bless all the tribes of the earth." But when God shall take me away from the world, Satan will raise again this accursed sedition, by making the impious believe that I am God and son of God, whence my words and my doctrine shall be contaminated, insomuch that scarcely shall there remain thirty faithful ones: whereupon God will have mercy upon the world, and will send his messenger for whom he hath made all things; who shall come from the south with power, and shall destroy the idols with the idolaters; who shall take away the dominion from Satan which he hath over men. He shall bring with them the mercy of God for salvation of them that shall believe in him, and blessed is he who shall believe his words.
Gospel of St. Barnabas
97: Muhammed is his blessed name

'Unworthy though I am to untie his hosen, I have received grave from God to see him'

then answered the priest, with the governor and the king, saying: 'Distress not thyself, O Jesus, holy one of God, because in our time shall not this sedition be any more, seeing that we will write to the sacred Roman senate in such wise that by imperial decree none shall any more call thee God or son of God.'

then said Jesus: 'With your words I am not consoled, because where ye hope for light darkness shall come; but my consolation is in the coming of the messenger, who shall destroy every false opinion of me, and his faith shall spread and shall take hold of the whole world, for so hath God promised to Abraham our father. And that which giveth me consolation is that his faith shall have no end, but shall be kept inviolate by God.' the priest answered: 'After the coming of the messenger of God shall other prophets come?'

Jesus answered: 'There shall not come after him true prophets sent by God, but there shall come a great number of false prophets, whereat I sorrow. For Satan shall raise them up by the just judgment of God, and they shall hide themselves under the pretext of my gospel.'

Herod answered: 'How is it a just judgment of God that such impious men should come?'

Jesus answered: 'It is just that he who will not believe in the truth to his salvation should believe in a lie to his damnation. Wherefore I say unto you, that the world hath ever despise the true prophets and loved the false, as can be seen in the time of Michaiah and Jeremiah. For every like loveth his like.'

Then said the priest: 'How shall the Messiah be called, and what sign shall reveal his coming?'

Jesus answered: 'The name of the Messiah is admirable, for God himself gave him the name when he had created his soul, and placed it in a celestial splendour. God said: "Wait Mohammed; for thy sake I will to create paradise, the world, and a great multitude of creatures, whereof I make thee a present, insomuch that whoso bless thee shall be blessed, and whoso shall curse thee shall be accursed When I shall send thee as my messenger of salvation and thy word shall be true, insomuch that heaven and earth shall fail, but thy faith shall never fail." Mohammed is his blessed name.'

Then the crowd lifted up their voices, saying: 'O God, send us thy messenger: O Mohammed come quickly for the salvation of the world!'
Gospel of St. Barnabas
103: Muhammed -the White Cloud of Mercy

Jesus went into the wilderness beyond Jordan with his disciples, and when the midday prayer was done he sat down near to a palm-tree, and under the shadow of the palm-tree his disciples sat down. Then Jesus said: 'So secret is predestination, O brethren, that I say to you, truly, only to one man shall it be clearly known. He it is whom the nations took for, to whom the secrets of God are so clear that, when he comes into the world, blessed shall they be that shall listen to his words, because God shall overshadow them with his mercy even as this palm-tree overshadows us. Yes, even as this tree protects us from the burning heat of the sun, even so the mercy of God will protect from Satan them that believe in the man.'

The disciples answered, "O Master, who shall that man be of whom you speak, who shall come into the world?" Jesus answered with joy of heart: 'He is Muhammed;, Messenger of God, and when he comes into the world, even as the rain makes the earth to bear fruit when for a long time it has not rained, even so shall he be occasion of god works among men, through the abundant mercy which he shall bring. For he is a white cloud full of the mercy of God, which mercy God shall sprinkle upon the faithful like rain.'

When Prophet Muhammed (u.w.b.p), took the Holy City of Makkan, without bloodshed, it was foretold viz;

"And this is the blessing wherewith Moses the man of God blessed the children of Israel before his death.

And he said, The Lord came from Sinal, and rose up from Seir unto them; he shined forth from mount Paran, and he came with the thousands of saints; from his right hand went a fiery law for them."22

in another place, it says;

"And Enoch also, the seventh from Adam, prophesied of these, saying, Behold, the Lord cometh with ten thousands of his saints,

To execute judgment upon all, and to convince all that are ungodly among them of all their ungodly deeds which they have ungodly committed, and of all their hare speeches which ungodly sinners have spoken against him."23

Prophet Muhammed (u.w.b.p), also known as the Paracelet or Comforter, is also mentioned in the Vedic Religion of India (misnomer-Hinduism).

Many Pundits of the Vedic Religion of India have considered the following, to be authentic. (see Khoorshid Khanum Ali Jairazbhoy-of Mumbai, Free Circulation Series #02, entitled: 'The Holy Prophet Muhammed Foretold in Ancient Scriptures'). The Prophecies are as follows;

"Just then and illiterate man with the epithet Teacher, Mahamad by name, came along with his companions Raja (Bhoja in a vision) so that Great Dava, the denizen of Arabia, purifying with the Ganges water and with the five things of cow offered sandal wood and pay worship to him.

O denizen of Arabia and Lord of the Holies to thee is my adoration.

O, thous who hast found many ways and means to destroy all the devils of the world. O pure one from among the illiterates, O sinless one, the spirit of truth and absolute master, to thee is my adoration.

Accept me at thy feet."24

In another prophecy, it says;

"O people, listen this emphatically! The man of praise (Muhammad will be raised among the people. We take the emigrant in our shelter from sixty thousand and ninety enemies whose conveyances are twenty camels and she camels, whose loftiness of position touches the heaven and lowers it.

He gave to Mamah Rishi hundred of gold coins, ten circles, three hundred Arab horses and ten thousand cows."25

In the Hadiths of Islam, the following is recordes;

Narrated by Abu Huraira (R.A).....

Allah's Apostle said: "On the night of my Ascension to Heaven, I saw (the prophet) Moses who was a thin person with lank hair, looking like one of the men of the tribes of Shanua, and I was Jesus who was of average height with a red face as if he had just come out of a bathroom.

And I resemble, Prophet Abraham more than any of his offspring does. Then I was given two cups, one containing milk and the other wine. Gabriel said,

'Drink whichever you like. 'I took the milk and drank it.

Gabriel said, 'You have accepted what is natural (True Religion i.e. Islam) and if you had taken the wine, your followers would have gone astray.'"26

In the Holy Book of Islam, the Holy Qur'an, Pro phet Muhammed (u.w.b.p), us mentioned numerous times. I have opted to mention only seven (7) places in this beautiful book, where this great personality is mentioned. In reference #28, Prophet Muhammed, is refered to as the Khatam-an-Nabiyyin or The Unlettered Prophet, meaning he could neither read nor write...

Another reason for meantioning these Qur'anic verses, is to highlight the fact, that Prophet Muhammed (u.w.b.p), also known as the Paracelete or Comforter, was sent to United Manking-Mentally, Physically and Spiritually against Gog and Magog and the Anti-Christ; to whom the next chapter is 'dedicated' to.

I have quoted seven(7) Qur'anic verses from the Holy Qur'an. These beautiful Seven verses are as follows:

O you who believe, obey Allah and obey the Messenger and those in authority from among you; then if you quarrel about anything, refer it to Allah and the Last Day. This is best more suitable in (achieve) the end.27

O People of the Book, indeed Our Messenger has come to you explaining to you after a cessation of the messenger, lest you say: There came not to us a bearer of good news nor a warner. So indeed a bearer of good news and a warner has come to you. And Allah is Possessor of power over all things.

Those who follow the Messenger-Prophet, the Ummi, whom they find mentioned in the Torah and the Gospel. He enjoins the good and forbids them evil, and makes lawful to themselves the good things and prohibits for them impure things, and removes from them their burden and the shackles which were on them. So those who believe in him and honour him and help him, and follow the light which has been sent down with him – these are the successful. 28

Say: O mankind, surely I am the Messenger of Allah to you all, of Him, Whose is the kingdom of the heavens and the earth. There is no god but He; He gives life and causes death. So believe in Allah and His Messenger, the Ummi Prophet who believes in Allah and His words, and follow him so that you may be guided aright.29
And whoever obeys Allah and the Messenger, they are with those upon whom Allah has bestowed favours from among the prophets and the truthful and the faithful and the righteous, and a godly company are they!30

He it is Who has sent His Messenger with the guidance and the Religion of Truth that He may make it prevail over all religions, through the polytheists are averse.31

Allah has promised to those of you who believe and do good that He will surely make them rulers in the earth as He will surely establish for them their religion, which He has chosen for them, and that He will surely give them security in exchange after their fear. They will serve Me, not associating aught with Me. And whoever is ungrateful after this, they are the transgressors.32

He it is Who has sent His Messenger with the guidance and the Religion of Truth that He may make it prevail over all religions. And Allah is enough for a witness.33

And to conclude this chapter on the subject of the Paraiete or the Comforter, please be reminded of what Prophet Jesus said;

"I indeed baptize you with water unto repentence: but that cometh after me is mightier than I, whose shoes I am not worthy to bear: he shall baptize you with Holy Ghost, and with fire."34

And he said, 'Take heed that ye be not deceived: for many shall come in my name, saying, I an Christ; and the time draweth near: go ye not therefore after them. But when ye shall hear of wars and commotions, be not terrified: for these things must first come to pass: but the end is not by and by.

Then said he unto them, Nation shall rise against nation, and kingdom against kingdom: And great earthquake shall be in drivers places, and famines, and pestilences; and fearful sights and great signs shall there be from heaven.'35

"For false Christs and false prophets shall rise, and shall show signs and wonders, to seduce, if it were possible, even the elect."36

(see also Gospel of Matthew 24:24)

The next chapter deals with – The Anti Christ or The Dajjal.

POSTSCRIPT

In Islam, Muslims are commanded and required to read the Holy Qur'an, from cover to cover, and in Arabic, however, if we're unable to read the Arabic them any temptation of it-whether in English, French, Greek or Islam also teaches us about, the Hadiths or the sayings and doing of Prophet Muhammed (u.w.b.p). The Hadiths are a manual for all followers of Islam to follow; it is also a guide of how to live life, day-by-day!

Enshrined in the Hadiths are Prophet Muhammed's sayings on the Dajjal or Anti-Christ. In the Appendix, I quoted some of the Hadiths regarding the Dajjal, and of which, I quoted from Mr. Ali Akbar's book, Prophecies of the Holy Qur'an.

The next page or two, I'm giving my readers (that's you), an opportunity, to read what the Hadiths, has to say, regarding, the Dajjal. The Hadiths are; Sahih Bukhari, Sahih Muslim and Sahih Abu Dawood.

Sahih Muslim; Ch. 21 Book 41 Numner 7025:
Abdullah bin Amr (R.A) reported: I committed to memory a hadith from Allah's Messenger (u.w.b.p) and I did not forget it after I had heard Allah's Messenger (u.w.b.p) as saying: The first sign (not of the signs of the appearance of the Dajjal) would be the appearance of the beast before the people in the morning and which of the two happens first, the second one would follow immediately after that.

Sahih Muslim; Ch. 18 Book 41 Number 7010:
Hadhalfa (R.A) reported that Allah's Messenger (u.w.b.p) said: Dajjal is blind of the left eye with thick hair and there would be a garden and a fire with him and his fire would be a garden would be fire.

Sahih Bukhari; Volume 03 Book 30 Number 103:
Narrated by Abu Bakr (R.A): The Prophet said, "The terror caused by Al-Masih Ad-Dajjal will not enter Medina and at that time Medina will have seven (7) gates and there will be two (2) angels at each gate guarding them."

Sahih Bukhari; Volume 04 Book 55 Number 555:
Narrated by Ibn Umar (R.A): Once Allah's Apostle stood amongst the people, gloried and praised Allah as he deserved and them mentioned the Dajjal saying, "I warn you against him (i.e. the Dajjal) and there was no propher but warned him nation against him. No doubt, Noah, warned his nation against him but I tell you about something of which no prophet told his nation before me. You should know that he is one-eyed, and Allah is not one-eyed."

Sahih Abu Dawood; Book 37 Number 4283:
Narrated by Abdullah ibn Busr (R.A), The prophet (u.w.b.p) said: The time between the great war and the conquest of the city (Constantinople) will be six (6) years, and the Dajal (Anti-Christ) will come forth in the seventh (7th.).
Sahin Anu Dawood; Book 37 Number 4305:

Narraged by Imran ibn Husayn (R.A), The Prophet (u.w.b.p) said:
Let him who hears of the Dajjal (Anti-Christ) go far from him for I swear by Allah that a man will come to him thinking he is a believer and follow him because of confused ideas roused in him by him.

Sahih Muslim; Ch 76 Book 01 Number 323:

It is narrated on the authority of Abdullah bin Umar (R.A), that the Messenger of Allah (u.w.b.p) said: I found myself one night near the Ka'bah, and I saw a man with wheat complexion amongst the fair-complexioned men that you ever saw. He had a lock of hair the most beautiful of the locks that you ever saw. He had combed it. Water was trickling out of them. He was leaning on two|(2) men, or on the shoulders of two(2) men, and he was circumscribing the Ka'bah. I asked, What is he? It was said: He is al-Masih, son of Mary. Then I saw another person, stout and having too much curly hair, and blind in his right eye as if it was a full swollen grape. I asked, Who is he? It was said: He is Al-Massih al Dajjal.

Even though, the Holy Qur'an doesn't mention directly, the Dajjal or Anti-Christ, it nevertheless mentions the disbelievers, who will meet their Creater on the day of Judgment, and who will know their fate!

Maulaana Muhammed Ali's translation and commentary of the Holy Qur'an, mentions the Anti-Christ or Dajjal in notes; 469, 1478, 1526 and 2195. The Anti-Christ or Dajjal, is one of three signs of the later days of mankind. The other two are: Dabbat al-ard and Gog and Magog.

The Holy Qur'an coincidentally, mentions alongside Gog and Magog, the historical personality of Dhu-l-Qarnain, who is known to the Christians as Darius I. (see Ezra 04:05, 24; 05:05; 06:01//Haggai 01:01;02:10//Zechariah 01:07//Nehemiah 12:22).

Dhu-l-qarnain is mentioned in the Holy Qur'an viz; Chapter 18 Verses 83 & 86 Notes; 1517, 1518 & 1519.

Gog and Magog is mentioned in the Holy Qur'an viz; Chapter 21 Verses 96 Notes; 1660 & 1661.

Both Dhu-l-qarnain and Gog and Magog is mentioned in the Holy Qur'an viz; Chapter 18 Verse 94 Note; 1523.

Maulaana Muhammed Ali, also wrote a world famous boo, entitled; The Anti-Christ and Gog and Magog.

This book was published by the Ahmadiyya Anjuman Isah' at Islam Inc., USA, ISBN: 0913321044. I request my readers to get a hold of this, 'Muhammed and Christ',, written by the above mentioned author.

ISBN: 0913321206. And to check out Chapter 03, Sections 01-03.

To my Readers, who purchased my book, I say to you, Thanks for engaging in a 'walk' down the hallway of History, Religion, Philosophy and Reality. Please continue reading, the Appendix section is next, because you'll be blown away, by the FACTS!

Aｐｐｅｎｄｉｃｅｓ

After the events of cross, a lot of misunderstanding arose, concerning Prophet Jesus.

Three (3) areas of contention viz:

1. Crucifixion
2. Dajjal and the Return of Jesus (a.s), son of Mary
3. Mary Magdalene

These areas of contention have caused strife within the Religion's of Islam and Christianity. Wars have been fought. Blood also has flowed, knee high to that of a horse's knee (First Crusade War). I would attempt to give a general outline of these three (3) topics.

CRUCIFIXON

Crucifixion was an ancient method of execution, in which the victim was tied or nailed to a large wooden cross and left to hang there until dead. Though closely associated with Rome, crucifixion originated with the Pheonicians and Persians. It was practiced from the 6th century BC until the 4th century A.D.
The Roman emperor Constantine I banned crucifixion in 337.

Crucifixion was hardly (if ever) performed for ritual or symbolic reasons; usually, its purpose was only to provide a particularly painful, gruesome and public death, using whatever means were most expedient for that goal.

The horizontal beam of the cross or transom could be fixed at the very top of the vertical piece, the upright, to form a (T), called a tall cross or Saint Anthony's Cross. The horizontal beam could also be affixed at some distance below the top, often in a mortise, to form a t-shape called a Latin Cross, most often depicted in Christian imagery

It also seems possible, that the Gospel accounts the-shape called a Latin Cross, most often depicted in Christian imagery.

It also seems possible, that the Gospel accounts the "alleged" death of Jesus, as a standard Roman procedure for crucifixion. Many a victims outstretched arms were affixed to the crossbar by either nails or ropes. (Prophet Jesus was nailed). This was then raised and secured at the perpendicular pole. Contrary to popular belief crosses were not high; the feet were probably only a few inches above the ground.

Death on the cross usually came slowly; it was not unusual for persons to survive for days on the cross. A person cannot die within a few hours of being on the cross or beam, two, their feet would have to be broken, exposure, diseases, hunger, shock and exhaustion were the usual immediate causes of death. In Prophet Jesus' case, he was a very healthy individual.

Bodies of the crucified were often left unburied and eaten by carnivorous birds and beasts, thus adding to the disgrace.

DAJJAL AND THE RETURN OF JESUS, SON OF MARY

The word Dajjal is derived from Dajjala, which means he covered (a thing). The Lisan-al-'Arab gives several views why Dajjal is so called.
1. He is so called on account of his being a liar and covering the truth with falsehood.
2. He will cover the earth with the largeness of his numbers.
3. He will cover the people with unbelief, and with his knowledge will discover things never before discovered.
4. He will spread over and cover the whole earth.

5. Dajjal is a community that will carry about its merchansdise all over the world, in other words he will cover the earth with its articles of trade.

6. Dajjal or Anti-Christ, was given this name because he will say things which are contrary to what is in his mind, simply say; he will cover his real intentions with false words.

Massih means Messiah, the sacred name given by Allah in the Holy Qur'an to the Prophet Jesus, and Dajjal will carry out his tasks in the name of the Holy man.

In the Book, Prophecies of the Holy Qur'an by Ali Akbar, Chapter 03, the following is meantioned:

"The true Messiah also preached that every man will stand before Allah and will be rewarded or punished according to his deeds. The Dajjal, however will preach that the son of Mary suffered sufficiently to cleanse the sins of the entire word and even Mary, the innocent mother of Jesus, is not free from the lies of Dajjal, and this is what is mentioned in saying that Dajjal is Anti-Christ."

There is vast collection of Hadiths(sayings and doings) of the Holy Prophet Muhammed, in which he foretold of the Trials and Tribulations of the Dajjal(Anti-Christ).He also spoke of Gog and Magog.The Hadiths tells us thus:

1. Our Holy Prophet Muhammed advised his followers that when the time comes and they must read first and the last ten verses of the chapter al-Kahf (The cave, Chapter 18) of the; Holy Qur'an, and they will be saved from his mischief, trails and tribulations of Dajjal.

(Ibn Massjah, 36:33; Abu Dawad, 36:14; Tirmidhi; 31-59; Musnad of Ahmad, Ch. 06, Vol. 01, p: 446)

The reason why the Holy Prophet Muhammad advised his followers to read these twenty verses of the Holy Qur'an was because these verses speak of the Christian disbeliefs, and, therefore there is not the least doubt that the tribulation Dajjal means the tribulation of the Christian nations or the materialistic civilization with which we are faced in the present day. And the name of Anti-Christ given to it is due to the fact that it is opposed to the true teaching of Christ, who never taught the doctrine of atonement. The Qur'an gives a clear warning against such a belief.

The purpose of the advent of the Prophet was:

"To warm those who say Allah has taken to himself a son." (ch. 18 verse 04)

Again:

"Do those who disbelieve think that they can take my servants to be friends besides me?" (ch. 18 verse 102).

And with regards to the materialistic outlook life we read in he Qur'an:

"Those, whose effort gives astray in this world's life, and they think that they are making good manufactures. (ch 18 verse 104)

1. The Holy Prophet Muhammed said: There is no trial and tribulation greater than that of Dajjal since the creation of man up to the coming of the Day or Resurrection.

   (Mishkaat al-Masaabih).

This can be seen if we look around the world at the poverty, hunger, persecution and cold-blooded murder; for surely there could be no more suffering that there is in the world today. And, as I can see in the results of memories of the two World Wars, the number of armed forces and civilian killed in these wars is vast; for even the number of those killed in the Second World War by conventional weapons and the atomic bombs totals several millions, and remembered (till) today. The Western leaders, when they talk of destroying human life, talk in terms of millions.

1. Whoever hears about Dajjal should keep away from him. By Allah! One will come to him and he will think that he is a believer, but he will follow him (Dijjal) on account of the boubts that he will raise in his mind.

4.   (Kanz-ul-'Ummaal, No. 2991).

As regards the above quotation, any true believing Muslim who has been in Contact with the European Christian Missionary abroad will clearly understand the way in which they work to gain converts.

Sweet talk, free gifts and promises and the smooth way in which their missionary schools are run, even if they cannot convert people to Christianity, they manage to put doubts in their minds and divert their own original faith.

My dear friends, Prophet Jesus (a.s.), came into this world by natural means and died by natural means, Prophet Jesus isn't coming a second time.

Instead someone with his characteristics shall come. I shall not go any further, trying to explain the Dajjal here are some Hadiths about Dajjal:

1. Sahih Muslim Hadith 7034, Narrated by Ana ibn Malik; Allah's Apostle (peace be upon him) said: The Dajjal would be followed by seventy thousand Jews of Isfahan wearing Persian shawls.

2. Sahih Al-Bukhari Hadith 9.505, narrated by Anas; The Prophet said: "Allah did not send any prophet but that he warned his nation of the one-eyed liar (ad-Dajjal). He is one-eyed while your Lord is not one-eyed. The word 'Kafir' (unbeliever) is written between his two eyes."

3. Sunan of Abu-Dawood Hadith 4311, narrated by Fatimah, daughter of Qay;

The apostle of Allah (peace be upon him) once delayed the congregation night prayer. He came out and said: Talk of Tamim ad-Dari detained me.

He transmitted to me from a man who was on of the island of the sea. All of a sudden he found a women who was trailing her hair, he asked: Who are you? She said, I am the Jassasah. Go to that castle. So I came to it and found a man who was trailing his hair, chained in iron collars, and leaping between Heaven and Earth. I asked: Who are you? He replied: I am Dajjal (Anti-Christ). Has the Prophet of the unlettered people come forth now? I replied: Yes. He said: Have they obeyed him or disobeyed him? I said: No, they have obeyed him. He said: That is better for them.

Sahih Muslim Hadith 6391, Narrated by Hudhayfah ibn Usayd Ghifari;

Allah's Apostle (peace be upon him) came to us all of a sudden as we are discussing about the last hour. Here upon he said: It will not come until you see ten signs before and (in this connection) he made a mention of the smoke, Dajjal, the beast, the rising of the sun from the West, the descent of Jesus, son of Mary (may Allah be pleased with him), The Gog and Magog, and landslides in three places, one in the east, one in the west and one in Arabia at the end of which fire would drive people to the place of their assembly.

To my Muslim sisters and brothers, there are many Islamic Scholars, who has written on the sensitive issue of the Dajjal. I ask you'll please collect a lot more information, from other great scholars on this subject, and be informed about the times that we're, currently in.

To my Christian Friends, I also ask you to collect as much information from the various distinguished Biblical Scholars who have written about the Anti-Christ, and whilst you read, you will see that, we live in the times, that are mentioned.

To my readers, the following book, is one that I recommend that you get:
THE NOSTRADAMUS CODE: WORLD WAR III
By Michael Rathford.
Distributed by Truth Revealed Publishing.
ISBN 9780977634101
MARY MAGDALENE

Is there any evidence in the Gospel and other before the Christianity, direct or indirect, that tells as that Prophet Jesus was married and could it be no lesser person that Mary Magdalene herself.

World renowned authors of – HOLY BLOOD, HOLD GRAIL, Mr. Michael Baigent, Mr. Richards Leigh and Mr. Henry Lincoln, states and their book, that Jesus was married to Mary Magdalene and that the marriage at Cana, for which the New Testament records him bearing some responsibility, was his own. I ask my readers, please get a hold of this book, and you investigate!

In Mr. Michael Baigent's book. THE JESUS PAPERS; he quoted from Mrs. Margaret Starbird's book, THE WOMAN WITH THE ALABASTER JAR, Concerning Mary Magdalene, "Starbird suggests that we can find the origins of Mary Magdalene in one of these prophecies. She points to the Old Testament prophet Micah (4:8), who wrote: 'And you, Tower of the Flock, Ophel of the daughter of Zion, to you shall be given back your former sovereignty, and royal power over the House of Israel.'

The phrase "Tower of Flock" means a high place from which the shepherd might watch over his flock. Here, though, according to the official Vatican translation (the Jerusalem Bible), it refers to Jerusalem.

The "Flock" refers to the faithful of God. The addition of the reference to "Ophel" reinforces this explanation, since Ophel was the district in Jerusalem where the King had his residence. As the Jerusalem Bible also explains, "Tower of the Flock" is Migdal-eder in Hebrew: Migdal means "tower", but it also carries the meaning of "great." Starbird suggests, very plausibly, that here we have the origins of the epithet "the Magdalene" rather then any possible town called Magdala. In other words, if this explanation is correct, Mary of Bethany, "the Magdalene", the wife of the Messiah, was known as "Mary the Great."

Mary Magdalene is mentioned fourteen (14) times in four (4) Gospels of the New Testament. She is also mentioned six (6) times in The Aquarian Gospel of Jesus the Christ. Her name is also mentioned in the Gospel of Philip in the Chapter entitled-"Wisdom of Magdala." Mary Magdalene, also had a Gospel named after herself, and it has five (5) Chapters.

In Dr. Barbara Thiering's book, JESUS: THE MAN. Turn to the Chapter entitled, People and Events – pages 393 & 394, we read:

"A member of the order of Dan, using the title 'Miriam', but in a branch of the order under Herodian influence, allowing divorce and remarriage. Her marriage to Jesus in AD 30 may have been her second.

Mary Magdalene was born in AD 3, and was aged 14 in AD 17 at the time she was "born" (the first initiation, at the age 14 for girls, 12 for boys). Older than usual at the time of her marriage, Mary Magdalene conceived in December AD 32, during the trial marriage. She had a daughter (Tamar) born in September AD 33, a son (Jesus Justas) born June AD 37, and a son in March AD 44."

AFTERWORD

This special Chapter is short but powerful. It contains some Kutbah's or sermons of Islam's Holy Prophet Muhammed (p.b.u.h)

The Prophet's First Khutbah in Madinah

All praise is due to Allah. I thank Him and seek His aid. I ask His forgiveness, and seek His guidance. I believe in Him and do not deny Him. I am the enemy of those who reject belief in Him. I bear witness that there is no one worthy of worship, other than Allah, Him alone, without partner; and that Muhammad is His servant and messenger whom He sent with guidance, true religion, light, and advice after a long gap of time when no messengers were sent, knowledge was little, people were misguided, and time appeared to have stopped as the Day of Judgment approached.

Whoever obeys Allah and His messenger is wise and whoever disobeys them is astray, wasted, and has lost his way far from the true path. I advise you to fear Allah and be conscious of Him. Be conscious of what Allah warned you of Himself. There is no better advice than that or a better reminder. It is a shield for those who follow this advice carefully and cautiously and it is an aid, and the truth that will get you what you aspire for on the Day of Judgment. Whosoever establishes a good relationship between him and Allah, secretly and openly, only to seek the pleasure of Allah, will benefit in this life and be saved in the afterlife when he will be in dire need of the good deeds he earned before death. Man will then wish that there were a great distance between him and anything else other than taqwa.

Allah warns you about Himself and He is kind to his servants. Allah, who has spoken the Truth and fulfilled his promise, has said: "I do not change My words and I do not oppress My servants" (50:29). Fear Allah in your present and future affairs, in secret and in the open for (Allah has said:) "Whosoever fears Allah, his sins will be forgiven and his reward will be many fold" (65:5) and "Whosoever fears Allah will achieve great success." Having taqwa (fearful awareness of Allah) protects man from Allah's anger, protects him from His punishment and protects him from His wrath. Taqwa illumines the face, pleases the Lord, and elevates the rank.

Take what is determined for you and do not neglect your relationship with Allah. He has taught you His book, laid down for you His path so that He will know which of you are the truthful and which of you are the liars. Therefore, do good, just as Allah has done good to you, and be enemies to His enemies, (for Allah has said:) "And strive in the way of Allah sincerely for He has chosen you and named you Muslims" (and "That those who have died (striving in His way) might die after a clear sign (had been given to them), and those who go on to live might live after a clear sign (had been given to them)" (8:42). There is no strength other than by Allah, thus increase the remembrance of Allah, and work for what will come after death, for whosoever builds a good relationship with Allah, Allah will protect him from the harm or need of people. Allah surely decrees what is destined for mankind, whereas they have no control over Him, and He has in store for them what they cannot have in store for Him. Allah is great. There is no power except by Allah, Elevated, the Great.

[End of first khutbah.]

The Prophet's Speech on the Importance of Knowledge.

Mu'ath bin Jabal narrated that the Prophet Muhammad, peace be upon him, said the following.

Acquire knowledge, for surely it leads to fear of Allah. Seeking it is an act of worship ('ibadah); studying it is praising Allah; seeking it is jihad; teaching it to whomever doesn't known it is an act of charity (sadaqah); and giving it to its people draws one closer to them. Knowledge points to the permissible (Halaal) and the forbidden (haraam); and it is a shining light pointing the way to paradise It comforts the lonely, befriends the estranged, and talks to you in seclusion. It is a guide through prosperity and adversity; it is a weapon against enemies; and it is the best of friends. With knowledge, Allah raises people to high stations, making them leaders in goodness, whose steps are traced. Their example is emulated, their opinion followed. The angels like to sit with the people of knowledge, surrounding their wings; and everything dry or wet, -fish of the sea and animals on land, - will ask Allah to forgive them. Knowledge gives life to the heart in the midst of ignorance, and illumines vision in the darkness.

With knowledge, God's servants become the elite and reach the highest degrees in this life and in the hereafter. Contemplation with knowledge is equivalent to fasting (sawm); spending time to study it is equivalent to standing at night in prayer (qiyam); duties to relatives are fulfilled by it; and through it the halaal and haraam are known. Knowledge precedes action ('amal) and action always follows it. The fortunate ones attain it and the miserable ones are deprived of it.

Christians and Jews

Muhammad once referred to strife, and said, "It will appear at the time of knowledge leaving the world." Ziad said, "O Messenger of God, how will knowledge go from the world, since we read the Kuran, and teach it to our children, and our children to theirs; and so on till the last day?" Then Muhammad said, "O Ziad, I supposed you the most learned man of Medinah. Do the Jews and Christians who read the Bible and the Evangel act on them?"

Do not exceed bounds in praising me, as the Christians do in praising Jesus, the son of Mary, by calling Him God, and the Son of God; I am only the Lord's servant; then call me the servant of God and His messenger.

When the bier of anyone passeth by thee, whether Jew, Christian or Muslim, rise to thy feet.

Prophet's Address at Tabuk

In 630 C.E., prophet Muhammad led an expedition to Tabuk. At Tabuk he delivered a classical address which provides glimpses of his message. After praising Allah T'ala and thanking Him, the Prophet said:

"Verily the most veracious discourse is the Book of Allah. The most trustworthy stronghold is the word of piety. The best of the religions is the religion of Ibrahim. The best of the precedents is the precedent of Muhammad. The noblest speech is the invocation of Allah. The finest of the narratives is this Quran. The best of the affairs is that which has been firmly resolved upon. The worst in religion are those things which are created without sanction. The best of the ways is one trodden by the Prophets. The noblest death is the death of a martyr. The most miserable blindness is the waywardness after guidance. The best of the actions is that which is beneficent. The best guidance is that which is put into practice. The worst blindness is the blindness of the heart.

The upper hand is better than the lower hand1. The little that suffices is better than what is abundant and alluring. The worst apology is that which is tendered when death stares one in the face. The worst remorse is that which is felt on the day of Resurrection.

Some men do not come to Friday prayer, but with hesitance and delay. And some of them do not remember Allah but with reluctance. The tongue which is addicted to false expression is a bubbling spring of sins.

The most valuable possession is the contentment of heart. The best provision is that of piety. The highest wisdom is fear of Allah, the Mighty and the Great. The best thing to be cherished in the hearts is faith and conviction; doubt is infidelity.

Impatient wailing and fulsome laudation of the dead is an act of ignorance. Betrayal leads one to the fire of Hell. Drinking amounts to burning. Obscene poetry is the work of the devil. Wine is the mother of all evil. The worst thing eaten is one which belongs to the orphan. Blessed is he who receives admonition from others.

Each one of you must resort to a place of four cubit (grave). Your affairs would be decided ultimately in the next life. The worst dream is false dream. Whatever is in store is near.

To abuse a believer is transgression; raising arms against him is infidelity. To backbite him is a disobedience of Allah. Inviolability (and sacredness) of his property is like that of his blood.

He who swears by Allah (falsely), in fact falsifies Him. He who pardons others is himself granted pardon. He who forgives others, is forgiven by Allah for his sins.

He who represses anger, Allah rewards him. He who faces misfortunes with perseverance, Allah compensates him. He who acts only for fame and reputation, Allah disgraces him. He who shows patience and forbearance, Allah gives him a double reward. He who disobeys Allah, Allah chastises him.

I seek the forgiveness of Allah.

I seek the forgiveness of Allah.

I seek the forgiveness of Allah.

FOOTNOTE

1. The hand which gives charity is better than the one which receives it. Reference: *Life of Muhammad* by Prof. A.H. Siddiqui, pp. 283-4

Prophet Muhammad's Last Sermon

Date delivered: 632 A.C., 9th day of Dhul al Hijjah, 10 A.H. in the 'Uranah valley of Mount Arafat.

After praising, and thanking God, he said: "O People, listen well to my words, for I do not know whether, after this year, I shall ever be amongst you again. Therefore listen to what I am saying to you very carefully and TAKE THESE WORDS TO THOSE WHO COULD NOT BE PRESENT HERE TODAY.

O People, just as you regard this month, this day, this city as Sacred, so regard the life and property of every Muslim as a sacred trust. Return the goods entrusted to you to their rightful owners. Treat others justly so that no one would be unjust to you. Remember that you will indeed meet your LORD, and that HE will indeed reckon your deeds. God has forbidden you to take usury (riba), therefore all riba obligation shall henceforth be waived. Your capital , however, is yours to keep. You will neither inflict nor suffer inequity. God has judged that there shall be no riba and that all the riba due to 'Abbas ibn 'Abd al Muttalib shall henceforth be waived.

Every right arising out of homicide in pre-Islamic days is henceforth waived and the first such right that I waive is that arising from the murder of Rabi'ah ibn al Harith ibn 'Abd al Muttalib.

O Men, the Unbelievers indulge in tampering with the calendar in order to make permissible that which God forbade, and to forbid that which God has made permissible. With God the months are twelve in number. Four of them are sacred, three of these are successive and one occurs singly between the months of Jumada and Sha'ban. Beware of the devil, for the safety of your religion. He has lost all hope that he will ever be able to lead you astray in big things, so beware of following him in small things.

O People, it is true that you have certain rights over your women, but they also have rights over you. Remember that you have taken them as your wives only under God's trust and with His permission. If they abide by your right then to them belongs the right to be fed and clothed in kindness. Treat your women well and be kind to them, for they are your partners and committed helpers. It is your right and they do not make friends with anyone of whom you do not approve, as well as never to be unchaste...

O People, listen to me in earnest, worship God (The One Creator of the Universe), perform your five daily prayers (Salah), fast during the month of Ramadan, and give your financial obligation (zakah) of your wealth. Perform Hajj if you can afford to.

All mankind is from Adam and Eve, an Arab has no superiority over a non-Arab nor a non-Arab has any superiority over an Arab; also a white has no superiority over a black nor a black has any superiority over white except by piety and good action. Learn that every Muslim is a brother to every Muslim and that the Muslims constitute one brotherhood. Nothing shall be legitimate to a Muslim which belongs to a fellow Muslim unless it was given freely and willingly. Do not, therefore, do injustice to yourselves.

Remember, one day you will appear before God (The Creator) and you will answer for your deeds. So beware, do not stray from the path of righteousness after I am gone.

O People, NO PROPHET OR MESSENGER WILL COME AFTER ME AND NO NEW FAITH WILL BE BORN. Reason well, therefore, O People, and understand words which I convey to you. I am leaving you with the Book of God (the QUR'AN*) and my SUNNAH (the life style and the behavioral mode of the Prophet), if you follow them you will never go astray.

All those who listen to me shall pass on my words to others and those to others again; and may the last ones understand my words better than those who listen to me directly. Be my witness O God, that I have conveyed your message to your people.

*The Qur'an: Revealed to Prophet Muhammad during the period from 610-632 AC. The first five verses revealed are: (1) Read in the name of your Lord, Who created. (2) Created man out of a clot that clings (in the womb). (3) Read and your Lord is the Most Bountiful. (4) Who taught by the pen. (5) Taught man that which he knew not.

And to conclude this special chapter, I wish to mention, The Dwellers I the cave.

The Holy Qur'an tells us thus:

Chapter 18 Verses 09-26

The head of state to whom the Dwellers had fled from was, Roman Emperor Gains Messius Quintus Decius (201-251). The Emperor was in charge of Empesus, which was an ancient Greek City on the West Coast of Anatolia, near present day selcuk, Izmir Province, Turkey.

The Seven (7) Sleepers were named thus;

1. Maximillian
2. Jamblichos
3. Martin
4. John
5. Dionysios
6. Exakostodianos
7. Antoninos

A stone tablet was made and the following inscription appeared on it;

"Commemoration of the seven (7) sleepers of Ephesus, who it is recounted, after undergoing martyrdom, rest in peace, awaiting the day of resurrection."

The aforementioned events appear in the following:

1. Greory of Tours . (b. 538 – d. 594)
2. Paul the Deron (b. 720 - d. 799); History of the Lombards
3. Jacobus de Voragine's, "Golden Legend (Legenda aurea)

My dear readers, some commentators have said that the Dwellers of the cave, slept for 187 years, other say, 357 years, Allah knows best!

And to conclude that chapter and my book, I leave you with the words of the Holy Qur'an, which are the words of Almighty Allah. Allah tells us thus:

6:19   Say: What thing is the weightiest in testimony? Say: Allah is witness between you and me. And this Quran has been revealed to me that with it I may warn you and whomsoever it reaches. Do you really bear witness that there are other gods with Allah? Say: I bear not witness. Say: He is only One God, and surely I am innocent of that which you set up (with Him).

قُلْ أَيُّ شَيْءٍ أَكْبَرُ شَهَادَةً قُلِ اللهُ شَهِيدٌ بَيْنِيْ وَبَيْنَكُمْ وَأُوْحِيَ إِلَيَّ هٰذَا الْقُرْاٰنُ لِأُنْذِرَكُمْ بِهِ وَمَنْ بَلَغَ أَئِنَّكُمْ لَتَشْهَدُوْنَ أَنَّ مَعَ اللهِ اٰلِهَةً أُخْرٰى قُلْ لَّا أَشْهَدُ قُلْ إِنَّمَا هُوَ إِلٰهٌ وَّاحِدٌ وَّإِنَّنِيْ بَرِيْءٌ مِّمَّا تُشْرِكُوْنَ ۩

10:37   And this Quran is not such as could be forged by those besides Allah, but it is a verification of that which is before it and a clear explanation of the Book, there is no doubt in it, from the Lord of the worlds.

وَمَا كَانَ هٰذَا الْقُرْاٰنُ أَنْ يُّفْتَرٰى مِنْ دُوْنِ اللهِ وَلٰكِنْ تَصْدِيْقَ الَّذِيْ بَيْنَ يَدَيْهِ وَتَفْصِيْلَ الْكِتٰبِ لَا رَيْبَ فِيْهِ مِنْ رَّبِّ الْعٰلَمِيْنَ ۩

19:83   Seest thou not that We send the devils against the disbelievers, inciting them incitingly?

أَلَمْ تَرَ أَنَّا أَرْسَلْنَا الشَّيٰطِيْنَ عَلَى الْكٰفِرِيْنَ تَؤُزُّهُمْ أَزًّا ۩

19:84   So make no haste against them. We only number out to them a number (of days).

فَلَا تَعْجَلْ عَلَيْهِمْ إِنَّمَا نَعُدُّ لَهُمْ عَدًّا ۩

19:85   The day when We gather the dutiful to the Beneficent to receive honours,

يَوْمَ نَحْشُرُ الْمُتَّقِيْنَ إِلَى الرَّحْمٰنِ وَفْدًا ۩

19:86   And drive the guilty to hell, as thirsty beasts.

وَنَسُوْقُ الْمُجْرِمِيْنَ إِلٰى جَهَنَّمَ وِرْدًا ۩

19:87   They have no power of intercession, save him who has made a covenant with the Beneficent.

لَا يَمْلِكُوْنَ الشَّفَاعَةَ إِلَّا مَنِ اتَّخَذَ عِنْدَ الرَّحْمٰنِ عَهْدًا ۩

19:88   And they say: The Beneficent has taken to Himself a son.

وَقَالُوا اتَّخَذَ الرَّحْمٰنُ وَلَدًا ۩

19:89   Certainly you make an abominable assertion!

لَقَدْ جِئْتُمْ شَيْئًا إِدًّا ۩

19:90   The heavens may almost be rent thereat, and the earth cleave asunder, and the mountains fall down in pieces,

تَكَادُ السَّمَوَاتُ يَتَفَطَّرْنَ مِنْهُ وَتَنْشَقُّ الْأَرْضُ وَتَخِرُّ الْجِبَالُ هَدًّا ۝

19:91   That they ascribe a son to the Beneficent!

أَنْ دَعَوْا لِلرَّحْمَنِ وَلَدًا ۝

19:92   And it is not worthy of the Beneficent that He should take to Himself a son.

وَمَا يَنْبَغِي لِلرَّحْمَنِ أَنْ يَتَّخِذَ وَلَدًا ۝

19:93   There is none in the heavens and the earth but comes to the Beneficent as a servant.

إِنْ كُلُّ مَنْ فِي السَّمَوَاتِ وَالْأَرْضِ إِلَّا آتِي الرَّحْمَنِ عَبْدًا ۝

19:94   Certainly He comprehends them, and has numbered them all.

لَقَدْ أَحْصَاهُمْ وَعَدَّهُمْ عَدًّا ۝

19:95   And everyone of them will come to Him on the day of Resurrection, alone.

وَكُلُّهُمْ آتِيهِ يَوْمَ الْقِيَامَةِ فَرْدًا ۝

19:96   Those who believe and do good deeds, for them the Beneficent will surely bring about love.

إِنَّ الَّذِينَ آمَنُوا وَعَمِلُوا الصَّالِحَاتِ سَيَجْعَلُ لَهُمُ الرَّحْمَنُ وُدًّا ۝

19:97   So We have made it easy in thy tongue only that thou shouldst give good news thereby to those who guard against evil, and shouldst warn thereby a contentious people.

فَإِنَّمَا يَسَّرْنَاهُ بِلِسَانِكَ لِتُبَشِّرَ بِهِ الْمُتَّقِينَ وَتُنْذِرَ بِهِ قَوْمًا لُدًّا ۝

19:98   And how many a generation before them have We destroyed! Canst thou see anyone of them or hear a sound of them?

وَكَمْ أَهْلَكْنَا قَبْلَهُمْ مِنْ قَرْنٍ هَلْ تُحِسُّ مِنْهُمْ مِنْ أَحَدٍ أَوْ تَسْمَعُ لَهُمْ رِكْزًا ۝

REFERENCES

Chapter 01: The Pious Family of Amran.

1. The Gospel of the Birth of Mary; 01:01-12
2. The Gospel of the Birth of Mary; 02:03-14
3. The Gospel of the Birth of Mary: 03:02-11
4. Holy Qur'an; 03:34-35
5. The Gospel of the Birth of Mary; 04:01-08

Chapter 02: The Virgin Mary and her Family.

1. Holy Qur'an; 19:18-21
2. The Gospel of the Birth of Mary; 07:03-17
3. The Gospel of the Birth of Mary; 05:02
4. The Gospel of the Birth of Mary; 05:04-17
5. Holy Qur'an: 03-43
6. The Gospel of the Birth of Mary; 07:01-07
7. Holy Qur'an; 03:41-46
8. Holy Qur'an; 19:16-26
9. The Aquarian Gospel of Jesus the Christ; 05:11-12
10. The Gospel of St. Barnabas: Chapter 06
11. The Aquarian Gospel of Jesus the Christ; 04:08-12
12. The Aquarian Gospel of Jesus the Christ; 05:18-12

Chapter 03: The Unknown Years of Prophet Jesus.

Chapter 04: The Prophet and his Ministry.

11. The Gospel of Matthew; 21:43

12. Holy Qur'an; 02:128-129

13. Holy Qur'an; 61:06

14. The Gospel of St. Thomas; 09:01-05

15. The Gospel of St. Thomas; 64:01-02

16. The Gospel of St. Thomas; 107:01-03

17. The Unknown Life of Jesus Christ; Chapter 09 Nos. 12-17

18. The Unknown Life of Jesus Christ: Chapter 10 Nos. 15-21

19. The Gospel of St.Barnabas;Chapter 37

20. The Gospel of Luke; 20:46-47

Chapter 05: An Event Unravelled.

1. The Gospel of Matthew; 21:10-11

2. The Gospel of Matthew; 26:03-05

3. The Gospel of Luke; 22:15-16

4. The Gospel of Mark; 14:18-21

5. The Aquarian Gospel of Jesus the Christ; 163:09-22

6. The Gospel of Luke; 22:41-46

7. The Gospel of Matthew; 26:42-45

8. The Gospel of John: 18; 2-3

9. The Gospel of John: 19:24

10. The Gospel of Matthew; 27:03-10

11. The Gospel of John 18:31

12. The Gospel of Luke; 23:02

13. The Gospel of John; 18-36

14. The Gospel of Luke; 23: 06-11

15. The Gospel of Luke; 23:13-16

16. The Aquarian Gospel of Jesus the Christ; 167: 44-49

17. The Gospel of Matthew; 27: 15-17

18. The Gospel of Matthew; 27:23

19. The Gospel of Matthew; 27: 24-25

20. The Gospel of Luke; 23; 24-25

21. Deuteronomy; 21:23

22. Holy Qur'an; 03:54

23. The Gospel of Matthew; 12: 39-40

24. Holy Qur'an; 37: 139-147

25. The Gospel of Nicodemus; Formerly called, The Acts of Pontius Pilate; 06: 22-23

26. The Gospel of Matthew; 27: 39

27. The Gospel of Matthew; 27: 41-42

28. The Gospel of Matthew; 27: 46

29. The Aquarian Gospel of Jesus the Christ; 171: 06

30. The Gospel of Nicodemus; Formerly called, The Acts of Pontius Pilate; 08: 07-08

31. The Gospel of Nicodemus; Formerly called, The Acts of Pontius Pilate; 07: 08

32. The Gospel of Matthew; 27: 63-66

33. The Gospel of Luke; 24: 25-26

34. The Gospel of Luke; 24: 37-46

Chapter 06: Migration to the Eastern Countries.

1. The Gospel of Luke; 04: 43

2. The Gospel of Luke; 19: 10

3. The Gospel of John; 10:16

4. The Acts of the Apostles; 09: 01-19

5. Rauzat-us-Safa; Volume 01: 132-133

6. Kanz-ul-Ummal: Volume 02: Page 71

7. Farhang-I-Asafiya: Volume 01 Page 91

8. Kanz-ul-Ummal: Volume 02 Page 71

9. Kanz-ul-Ummal: Volume 02 Page 51

Chapter 07: Paraclete.

1. The Gospel of John; 14:16
2. The Gospel of John; 25:26
3. The Gospel of John; 15: 26
4. The Gospel of John; 16: 07-08
5. The Gospel of John; 16: 12-14
6. The Gospel of Matthew; 12: 31-32
7. The Gospel of Matthew; 21: 43
8. Deuteronomy; 18: 18
9. Holy Qur'an; 61: 06
10. Genesis; 17: 20
11. Genesis; 21: 18 & 21
12. Holy Qur'an; 14: 37
13. 1 Chronicles; 32-33
14. Isaiah; 07: 14-15
15. Song of Solomon; 08-16
16. 2 Chronicles; 32-33
17. Isaiah; 42: 10-11
18. Habakkuk; 03: 03-07
19. Psalms 72
20. Isaiah 60
21. Isaiah; 21: 07 & 13-17
22. Deuteronomy; 33: 01-02
23. Epistle of Jude: 14-15
24. Bhavishya Purana; Parv 03 Khand 03 Adya 03 Sholok 05-08
25. Atharva Veda; Khanda 20 Sukta 127 Mantra 01-03
26. Sahih Bukhari; Volume 04 Book 55 Number 607

27. Holy Qur'an; 04: 59

28. Holy Qur'an; 05: 19

29. Holy Qur'an; 07:157-158

30. Holy Qur'an; 04: 69

31. Holy Qur'an; 09: 33

32. Holy Qur'an; 24: 55

33. Holy Qur'an; 48: 28

34. The Gospel of Matthew; 03: 11

35. The Gospel of Luke; 21: 08-11

36. The Gospel of Mark; 13: 22

BIBLIOGRAPHY

Among the Dervishes by O.M. Burke, Octagon Press Ltd., 1993. Atharva Veda: Sacred Text of the Vedic Religion and one (1) of four (4) vedas or books of Knowledge. (see, "The Hymns of Atharva Veda", Translation by Ralph T.H. Griffith)

Bhavishva Mahapurane: One of the Eighteen (18) Major Text of the Vedic Religion, that tells of ancient times.

Concept of God in Major Religions by Dr. Zakir Naik. Islamic Research Foundation.

Glimses of World History by Pandit Jawahar Lal Nekru. ISBN: 0143031058.

Jesus in India by Hadhrat Mirza Ghulam Ahmad. Islam International Publications Ltd., 1995.

Jesus The Man by Dr. Barbara Thering. Atria Books (Simon & Schuster). 2006. Kanz-ul-Ummal: Hadith Collection of Islam.

Rauzat-us-Safa by Muhammad bin Khawendshah bin Mahmud. Reprinted by Kessinger Publishing LLC

The Aquarian Gospel of Jesus The Christ. Transcribed from, "The Book of God's Remembarance   (Akashic Records)" by Levi H. Dowling (1844-1911). Adventures Unlimited Press. 1908.

The Crucifixion by an Eyewitness. Published by the Indo-American Book Co. of Chicago.

The Fifth Gospel by Fida Hassnain and Dahan Levi. Blue Dolphin Publishing, 2006.

The Gospel of the Birth of Mary. Anonymous. Translated by William Wake from, "The Supressed Gospels and Epistle of the Original New Testament of Jesus Christ."

The Gospel of Barnabas. Text and Commentary taken from ww.barnabas. net., A member of The Sabr Foundation.

The Gnostic Gospels of Jesus by Marvin Meyer, Harper Collins (USA) 2005.

The Holy Bible. King James Version. World Bible Publishers.

The Holy Qur'an. Translation and Commentary by Maulaana Muhammed Ali.

Ahmadiyya Anjuman Isha'at Islam Inc., USA 1994.

The Jesus Papers by Michael Baigent. Harper Collins Publishers (UK), 2006.

The Trial of Jesus of Nazareth by Professor S.G.F Brandon. Dorset Press, 1968.

The Unknown Life of Jesus Christ by Nicholas Notovitch. Dragon Key Press, 2005.

ABOUT THE AUTHOR

Wazir Kooloo is a Government Field Officer, attached to a Division of the Ministry of Health, of the Government of Trinidad and Tobago.

A Tailor by Trade and an avid cricket fan. The author is true patriot of his homeland, cause he loves the cuisine and culture of this twin island state, that he calls home!

The author coincidentally resides in one of Trinidad and Tobago's historic Communities, which has the island's first Presbyterians Church and the first Mosque, both built in 1868.

The author is a member of the Islamic Sect that the world knows as the Ahmadiyya Anjuman Isha'ati-Islam Inc. (Trinidad and Tobago).

The author considers himself a student of World History, Philosophy and Comparative Religion.

He is therefore dedicating this book, to all members of the Ahmadiyya Sect of Islam (world-wide), who are heckled, humiliated, arrested, persecuted and even tortured on a daily basis.

The author wants to remind them, that the jihad (struggle), will continue, but, emancipation will come.....................